Encounters
Abroad

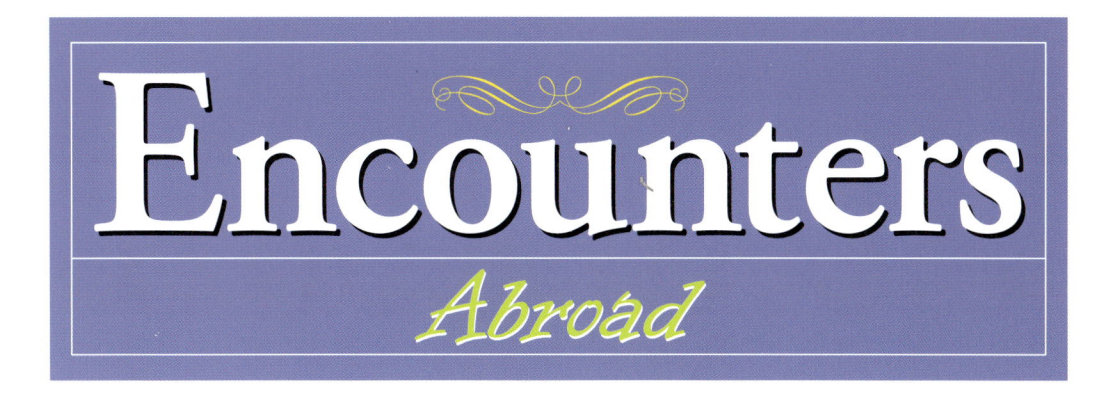

Michael P. Critchley

NAN'UN-DO

Acknowledgements

Encounters Abroad
by
Michael P. Critchley

©2007 All Rights Reserved

Acknowledgements

The author would like to thank the students at Josai International University (JIU) for their cooperation, feedback and patience during the development of this textbook. My apologies for all the times I had to re-teach an activity after realizing it just didn't work and needed revision.

A very special thanks to the students of the pilot groups. From the Matsuo group, Mieko Akiba, Masako Suzuki, Yukiko Kitada, Atsuko Hanazawa, Yoshiko Koyasu, Ayaka Sato, Keiko Hanazawa, Reiko Mamiya, Tomoko Hirayama and Yachiyo Otsuka. And from the JIU groups, Kaori Shoji, Haruka Furuya, Keita Asada, Ryutaro Hiroki, Kazuki "Ska" Sugai, Ryuta Suzuki, Yuko Tashiro, Kaoru Abe, Saki Shimabukuro, Yukino Maeyama and Hitomi Naito.

A very special thank you also to Aldo Villarroel, who was bold enough to take the first draft of the book into a pilot class. My apologies for any inconvenience this caused, and my thanks for the very helpful feedback. My sincere thanks also to Lori Parish and Kelly Ise, who kindly gave their time and their voices to the CD pilot recordings. Thanks to Miyuki Hatori for help in finding Canadian bills to photograph. Special thanks also to Jim Knudsen for his very professional final edit of the English Edition, and also my thanks to Jason Anderson for his expertise in doing the final touch ups on the cover design.

Thanks also to (in order of appearance) Bansei "Haru" Newcomb, Hitoshi Fukushima, Mako Kitamura, Takeshi Usuda, Corey Newcomb, Martha Yamamoto, Mei Wakabayashi, and Yuki Fukushima for allowing their images to be used in the unit cover photos. Thanks also to David Harding, Jr. for assistance with the photography. Further specific acknowledgements can be found in the back cover of this book.

I am deeply indebted to Taisuke Aoki, Yoshi Katagiri and the publishing team at NAN'UN-DO for their support and patience in this latest *Encounters* project. Thanks also to our illustrator, Sato Yusaku. As always, it has been a pleasure working with you all.

To the Chancellor of JIU, Dr. Noriko Mizuta, and to the administration of JIU, I would like to express my deepest appreciation for your continued support and cooperation in this endeavor.

Finally, a very special thank you to Maria Shiguemi Ichiyama, a cowriter of *Encounters* Books 1 and 2, my friend and colleague, and now my boss. Your dedication to this field has been and will continue to be a true inspiration. For the innumerable ways in which you've helped and supported me, I can only say, *muito obrigado*.

To the Student

学生の皆さんへ

Encounters Abroad にようこそ！このテキストの名前は「海外での出会い」という意味です。皆さんが海外に行く際、さまざまな「出会い」の中で、英語でより上手にコミュニケーションができるように願って、このテキストを作りました。

Encounters Abroad の特徴

1. この教科書の１０ユニットでは、カナダへの旅行がテーマとなり、旅に必要な英語が旅行の順番通りに提供されます。飛行機に乗ってから、入国手続き、ホテルまでのタクシー、チェックイン、観光アドバイス、車のレンタル、道案内、ショッピング、友達を誘う、そして最後には、外食の場面があります。この共通テーマがありますので、内容はより覚えやすく、実際に旅行するときにも、思い出せます。

2. 旅行英語なので、国内のホテル、空港、レストランなどで働いている人、働きたい人にとっても役に立つでしょう。

3. 旅行英語だけではなく、より社交的な英会話も含まれています。例えば、旅行中に人と出会う際、どういう風に話せば、誘えば、そして自分のことについて話せばいいのか、丁寧に教えます。

4. このテキストの中の会話は暗記して覚える必要がいっさいありません。モデル会話を読んで、どういう風に、どういう流れで会話すればいいのかを勉強してから、自分の言葉で話せるようになることを、各ユニットの最終目標にしています。

5. 日本語版では、要点だけではなく、各説明も日本語で書かれています。すぐに理解して、なるべく多くの時間を、実際に英語を使って話す練習にあてて欲しいからです。

Encounters Abroad を使った英語上達法

- 宿題、予習や復習を必ずしましょう。

- CDを効果的に使いましょう。はじめに、テキストを見ながらCDを聞き、声を出して練習します。次に、テキストを見ないでCDを聞き、各セリフの後に声を出して言ってみます。この時、発音をまねることがとても大切です。iPODやその他のMP3プレーヤを持つ人には、このCDをダビングし、暇な時にも聞けます。

- 自分が十分に理解しているかどうか、自分の学習について意識をする習慣をつけましょう。わからないところがあったら、すぐ先生に質問しましょう。

- 各ユニットの最後にある自己評価表を使い、自分の英語の上達を必ずチェックしましょう。

- 皆さんが授業外で英語を使う機会は、おそらく限られているでしょう。だからこそ、ペアワークなど授業中の練習時間を最大限に生かし、クラスメイトや先生とのコミュニケーションに積極的に参加しましょう。

I hope you enjoy studying with *Encounters Abroad*.
Mike Critchley

To the Teacher

About this book

Welcome to **Encounters Abroad**, the third volume in the *Encounters* series of speaking and listening coursebooks. This lower to upper-intermediate level text explicitly prepares learners for situation-based communication abroad, with a secondary focus on general casual conversation. There are three editions of **Encounters Abroad**:

Japanese Edition (Standard): New words and phrases translated. All language explanations given in Japanese.

English Edition: New words and phrases translated. All other text material in English.

Teacher's Edition: English edition with all answers written directly in the text.

Student learning is supported by the attached mini-phrasebook and the CD, on which all of the dialogues are recorded. Listening transcripts can be found on page 92. This textbook also incorporates Japanese language support so that teachers spend less time explaining and students spend more time communicating.

There are 10 units in this book, each built up around a travel-related situation within the broader context of a trip to Canada. This ongoing theme facilitates student understanding, and helps them to subsequently recall key language during real-life communication. This contextual strand is mirrored in the two unit reviews, where students move through extended role plays of simulated trips to Los Angeles and San Francisco.

I chose Canada as the setting for the book because of its popularity as a tourist destination and also because it is my home country, and thus gives me the greatest access to information and realia. However, this textbook does not "teach" Canadian culture, nor does it draw upon local slang or dialect (there is not one "*eh*" in the book). As such, it is a book that deals with language and settings that students will be able to apply to any country they choose to visit. I considered using a variety of international settings, but in the end, the need to create an ongoing contextual theme seemed more important.

Unit organization

This textbook takes a genre-based approach to learning. Each unit begins with the statement of an explicit social, communicative objective. Students are shown a model conversation of how an advanced speaker might achieve this objective. They then practice language pattern and communication points that directly support this objective. The final assessment section of each unit gives students the opportunity to create and carry out a similar conversation in their own words. At no point are they expected to memorize model conversations.

Although the units are designed to be modular, new vocabulary and language points are introduced in *every* unit, and there is a significant amount of recycling as the book progresses. I therefore recommend that you try to teach in the sequence offered in this book, even if you decide to skip a few units.

Each unit is organized around the following main sections.

- **Warm-up Questions and Unit Objective**

Each unit starts off with three general questions related to the unit's topic and theme. These questions lead naturally to the unit's primary objective, which specifically states what students should be able to do by the end of the unit. In more advanced classes, these questions can serve as the catalyst for a stimulating teacher-student discussion session.

To the Teacher

• Warm-up Listening
Students listen to a conversation and answer two warm-up listening questions. The first is an easier "listen and check" type question, and the second a more challenging "listen and write" question. Even in classes where the level of student ability varies, all students should be able to participate to some degree.

• Model Conversation
The model conversation allows students to see how the unit's language focus, vocabulary, and communication points might look when assembled and used in a complete conversation. New unit vocabulary is presented in the form of a marginal gloss.

• Language Focus
Students study two grammar or vocabulary points that directly support the unit objective. When appropriate, these points are intentionally recycled in future units. It is strongly recommended that teachers assign these two pages as homework before starting a new unit.

• Communication Focus
Students work through the main functional stages of the unit conversation. This section both mirrors and analyzes the model conversation, breaking it down into its key components. After completing this section, students should know how to reassemble the stages of the conversation and have the tools they require to achieve the unit objective.

• Role Play
Whether you use these role plays or develop situations of your own, you need to make sure that students work through a complete conversation from beginning to end. Higher-level students can be challenged further by incorporating the Challenge Role Play into the regular role-play situation. This "strategic" role play introduces a problem that students need to deal with spontaneously on their own without prior prompting or practice.

• Self Assessment Role Play: Over to you!
In this section, students are asked to prepare their own role play. Very little guidance is given in order to encourage independent study and creativity. Following this role play is a checklist of the major points covered in the unit. Students use the list to monitor and assess their own learning. This provides students with explicit evidence of their own learning gains, which builds confidence and promotes motivation.

Thank you for choosing **Encounters Abroad**. I sincerely hope that you find it a useful teaching and learning tool. For quizzes, an on-line teacher's manual and other teacher resources, please visit the *Encounters* web site. Comments and suggestions welcome.

http://www.encounters.jp

How to Use Encounters Abroad

Timing of the course

Encounters Abroad is designed to be taught over 36 class hours. Plan on using three hours (two 90-minute classes) per unit, one class for each of the two review units, and the remaining classes for midterms or review. Although teachers will naturally add to or subtract from this book according to their individual needs and styles, a typical unit might be broken down as follows.

	Content to cover	Time required	Teaching points
Home work	Language Focus	As homework	Assign the next unit's language focus as homework. Since language points and exercise instructions are written in Japanese, students can typically figure these pages out on their own.
CLASS 1	• Warm-up Questions • Unit Objective • Warm-up Listening	15 minutes	Start the unit with the warm-up questions and objectives to immerse students in the theme and goals of the unit. Warm-up listening can be done as a warm-up, or at the end of the unit as a consolidation and reinforcement exercise.
	• Model Conversation	15 minutes	Highlight the marginal gloss with some choral pronunciation. Allow students to read the conversation in pairs, then have them answer the activity question. Finally, read chorally with the class. Use the conversation recorded on the CD either before or after student practice, or assign it as listening homework.
	• Language Focus	30 minutes	Have selected students write their homework answers on the board. Correct with minimal commentary so the class can move on to the next section as quickly as possible. Provide supplementary practice as required.
	• Communication Focus	30 minutes	Give choral practice of the examples, and model speaking activities with students to demonstrate what they need to do. Complete in CLASS 2 if necessary. (If you use the Japanese edition, you won't require a lot of class time for explanation.)
CLASS 2	• Role Plays	30-45 minutes	Have students perform the role plays. Provide plenty of encouragement and support, emphasizing positive performance aspects. If class time is limited, cut the role plays short and move on to the original role play below.
	• Self-Assessment Role play & Checklist	To end of class	This is a crucial part of the unit. Students role play situations they create on their own using language that is (one hopes) appropriate to context. Be sure all students use the checklist at some point during the role plays. This promotes independent learning as students judge their own performance.

Unit evaluation

To assign a numerical value to student performance, teachers can create their own point system or download the evaluation sheets from the *Encounters* web site. Some teachers prefer to assess student-teacher role plays, others prefer to rate students during pair work. In either case, the bulk of course evaluation should be based on oral assessment. This raises the importance of oral production in the eyes of students, creating a powerful washback effect that influences what and how they study and learn.

Regarding unit evaluation, any student who can complete the communicative objective *at their level* should be rewarded with a good grade. While lower-level students can be rewarded even if they learn only the basic functional language presented, higher-level students can be expected to converse with more finesse and to use a greater amount of unrehearsed language. As long as learners know what you expect from them on an individual basis, they will feel that your grading is fair.

Table of Contents

Acknowledgements	2
To the Student	3
To the Teacher	4
How to Use Encounters Abroad	6

Unit 1	Unit 2	Unit 3	Unit 4	Unit 5
8	16	24	32	40
Where Are You Heading?	*May I See Your Passport?*	*Where To?*	*I Asked for a Double*	*What Would You Suggest?*
Talk about yourself and your travel plans when meeting a stranger	Fill out a landing card and answer questions at immigration	Take a taxi, give directions, and chat with the driver en route	Reserve a hotel room online and deal with problems at check in	Talk about interests when asking for sightseeing advice
• Asking about plans: planning to/going to • Expressing plans: going to/probably/ might	• Talking about future plans: Will be ~ing • Making requests: Can you/Could you	• Using let • Talking about prices; Photos of US and Canadian currency	• Completing online reservation forms • Solving problems: I was told that I asked for	• Expressing interests: I'd like to • Making suggestions: I'd suggest You could

Unit 6	Unit 7	Unit 8	Unit 9	Unit 10
50	58	66	74	82
Here Are Your Keys	*Turn Left at the Light*	*How Much Is This?*	*Are You Free Tomorrow?*	*I'll Have the Steak*
Select and rent a car, filling out necessary rental forms	Meet and chat with a stranger when asking for directions	Talk about items and negotiate prices when shopping	Call and invite a friend, arrange times and give directions	Read a menu, discuss food, order, then give opinions about food
• Filling out a rental agreement • Filling out a vehicle ready report	• Imperative • Direction commands: Turn left Go straight	• Complaints: It's a little loose. • Comparisons: Do you have a larger size?	• Embedded questions: Do you know where~is? • Simple directions: It's just beside there.	• Reading menus • Using the, a and some with menu items

Unit Review 1: Units 1 - 5		Unit Review 2: Units 6 - 10	
48		90	
Simulate a sightseeing trip to Los Angeles		Simulate a side-trip to San Francisco	
• Small talk en route	• Check in	• Rent a car	• Invite a new friend to dinner
• Immigration	• Sightseeing around LA	• Ask directions	• Dinner with friends
• Taxi to hotel		• Shop	

Listening transcripts	92

1 Where Are You Heading?

Have you ever spoken with a foreigner?[1]

How can you start a conversation with a stranger?

What topics do you talk about when you meet somebody new?

国際旅行では、毎日のように外国人とコミュニケーションをすることになります。このユニットでは、人と初めて出会う設定で、自分のことや旅行の計画について話す練習をします。

Warm Up...

[1] a foreigner 外国人
foreign 外国の〜

Mai は Vancouver 行きの飛行機に乗るため、成田空港で待っています。ラウンジに空いている席を見つけ、その席が空いているか隣の人に尋ね、会話が始まります。彼らの会話を聞き、次の質問に答えましょう。

Question 1: Mai がカナダでする予定を3つ下にチェックしましょう。

☐ play tennis   ☐ go fishing   ☐ work part-time   ☐ go sailing

☐ visit a friend   ☐ go skiing   ☐ see a hockey game   ☐ study English

Question 2: 次の質問に答えてください。

1. Where does Bob work? _____

2. Where is Mai from? _____

3. What does Mai study in Japan? _____

8 Encounters Abroad

Model Conversation

Meeting people en route[1]

Masashiは、成田から、カナダのバンクーバー行きの飛行機に乗ったところです。隣の乗客と会話を始めます。旅行の計画や一般的な個人情報について二人が話をします。

Activity 1 Read the conversation below with a partner. Underline the things that Masashi plans to do in Canada.

Masashi: I hope[2] it's a smooth[3] flight today.

Karen: Yeah, me, too. My flight to Japan was a bit rough.[4]

Masashi: So...are you from Vancouver?

Karen: No, I'm from Victoria.

Masashi: No way! Really?[5] That's where I'm heading.[6]

Karen: Oh, really? Great. So...what are you planning to do in Victoria?

Masashi: Well, for the first few days, I'm going to do some sightseeing.[7] Then, after that,[8] I'm going to go camping with a friend.

Karen: Oh, that sounds great.[9]

Masashi: Yeah, and if I have time, I might go to the Rocky Mountains. Actually,[10] I want to go skiing, too, but I don't think I'll have enough money.

Karen: Yeah, it *is* expensive.[11]

Masashi: Well, we'll see how things go.[12] So...do you live downtown?[13]

Karen: No, I'm from a place called Langford. It's about 30 minutes north of Victoria.

Masashi: I see. So...what do you do?

Karen: I work at a hospital. How about you? What do you do?

Masashi: Oh, I'm a student.

Karen: Oh, yeah. What's your major?[14]

Masashi: Marketing.

Karen: No way! Really? My father's in marketing. By the way,[15] my name is Karen.

Masashi: Hi, Karen. I'm Masashi. Nice to meet you.

Karen: Yeah, nice to meet you, too. Oh! Here we go![16]

---

[1] en route 目的地に行く途中
[2] I hope 〜だといい
[3] smooth スムーズな
[4] rough スムーズではない／揺れている
It was a bit rough 結構揺れていた
[5] No way! Really? まさか！（本当に？）
[6] to head (to) に向かう
That's where I'm heading ちょうど私が向かっている場所ですね。
[7] to do some sightseeing 観光する
[8] Then, after that そして、その後
[9] That sounds... 〜そう
That sounds great 楽しそうですね。
[10] Actually... 実は、
[11] expensive（値段が）高い
[12] We'll see how things go. 様子をみて、考えます。
[13] downtown 都市の中心部
[14] a major 専攻／専門
[15] By the way ところで
[16] Here we go! 出発進行！

Unit 1 9

Language Focus

Asking about future plans

[1] to stay 泊まる／いる
[2] an airline 航空会社
[3] a semester 学期
[4] How long... どれ位（の時間）～
[5] Where else... その他にどこに～

これからの予定について話をするときに、**going to**（～する予定）や**planning to**（～するつもり）は、よく使われます。一般的な会話では、どちらを使っても同じ意味になります。

Asking about future plans	
Are you **going to** go skiing tomorrow? （明日スキーに行く予定ですか。）	No, I can't go. I have to work.
What **are** you **planning to** do in Hokkaido? （北海道で何をするつもりですか。）	I'm going to visit a friend in Hakodate, then I'm planning to go to Furano.

Language Exercise 1: 単語を並べ替え、疑問文を作ってください。そして、各質問に対して自分の考えを書きましょう。

1. (are / next weekend / stay[1] / in Kyushu / you / planning to)

   Question: _____

   You: _____

2. (planning to / are / to Tokyo / when / you / go / with your friends)

   Question: _____

   You: _____

3. (airline[2] / going to / are / use / what / you)

   Question: _____

   You: _____

4. (you / next semester[3] / take / are / an English class / going to)

   Question: _____

   You: _____

Language Exercise 2: 外国人の友人は、"**I'm going to go to Hokkaido next month**"と言います。その旅について、あなたが聞きたい質問を書きましょう。そして、パートナーとその質問を聞いたり、答えたりしましょう。

1. Where _____

2. How long[4] _____

3. Are _____

4. What _____

5. Where else[5] _____

6. _____

Language Focus

[1] while ～の間
while you're there あなたがそこにいる間

Expressing future plans

旅行の予定やその他の未来の予定について話をする場合は、その予定がどの程度確実かを表現しなければなりません。下の表現は、会話でよく使われます。

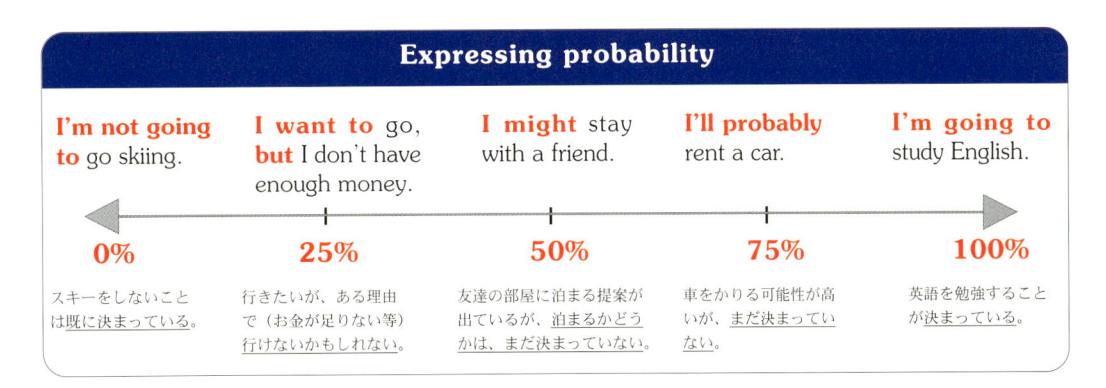

Expressing probability				
I'm not going to go skiing.	**I want to** go, but I don't have enough money.	**I might** stay with a friend.	**I'll probably** rent a car.	**I'm going to** study English.
0%	25%	50%	75%	100%
スキーをしないことは既に決まっている。	行きたいが、ある理由で（お金が足りない等）行けないかもしれない。	友達の部屋に泊まる提案が出ているが、泊まるかどうかは、まだ決まっていない。	車をかりる可能性が高いが、まだ決まっていない。	英語を勉強することが決まっている。

Language Exercise 3: ( )内の主語や動詞と、可能性を表す赤いパーセントと合わせて、文を完成させましょう。

Dan: So...what are you planning to do this summer?

Mari: Actually, (I / go / 100%) _____ to California.

Dan: No way! Really? That's great. So...what are you planning to do there?

Mari: (I / meet / 100%) _____ a friend of mine who lives in Riverside. (we / rent / 75%) _____ a car and travel around and, you know, do some sightseeing.

Dan: That sounds great. So...are you going to study English while[1] you're there?

Mari: (I / take English classes / but.../ 25%) _____

_____

How about you? What are you going to do this summer?

Dan: Well, I'm not sure yet. (I / go back / 0%) _____ to England, so (I / head / 50%) _____ to Kyushu.

Language Exercise 4: 上の表現を使い、今度の週末の予定について書きましょう。そして、"**So...what are you planning to do this weekend?**" とパートナーに質問し、週末の予定について話し合ってみましょう。

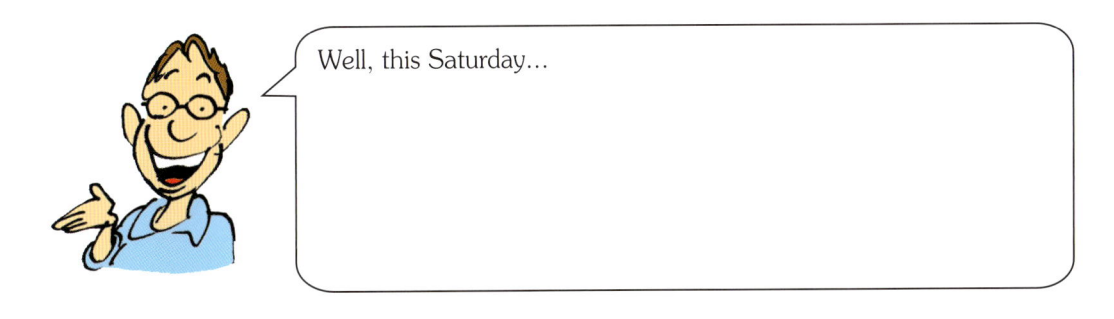

Well, this Saturday...

Unit 1　11

Communication Focus

Meeting people when traveling

初対面の人と初めて会話をするときに、二人が一緒にいる状況についてコメントを言うことによって、会話をスムーズに始めることができます。例えば、9頁のモデル会話では、Masashi が Karen に "I hope it's a smooth flight today" と、会話のきっかけとして話しかけています。

Activity 2 For each situation below, write what you could say to start a conversation.

Situation	Comment
1. 電車のチケットを買うため、あまり動いていない長い列に並んでいます。隣に立っている外国の人がアイコンタクトをしてきます。	
2. あなたは飛行機に座っています。もう一時間も待っているのに、飛行機が離陸せず、アナウンスもまだされていません。	

Talking about travel

旅行者の多くは、旅行についての話を好みます。例えば、モデル会話では、Masashi が Karen と一緒に彼のカナダでの計画について話します。

Activity 3 Use the Internet or travel guides to plan a two-week trip to a country you would like to visit. What are you going to do? Fill in the blanks below.

1. Well, I'm going to _____

2. I'll probably _____

3. I might _____

4. I want to _____ ,
   but _____

相手の旅行計画について質問をして、それに対するコメントを言いましょう。相手の旅先についてあなたが詳しいなら、アドバイスも言いましょう。

Activity 4 You are in a long line at a travel agency. Begin talking with the person beside you. Use the information from Activity 3 to talk about your trip. Make comments and ask questions.

- No way! Really? So...how long are you planning to stay there?
- Well, it's really cold there, so dress warm!
- Oh, yeah? So...where are you going to go to school?
- You should also visit the museum there. It's great!

Communication Focus

Talking about personal information

初対面の場合、自分のことについて話すのが普通です。自分の出身地、仕事あるいは勉強についての話をしてみましょう。相手の興味を引くような面白い情報も伝え、会話が続くようにしましょう。

Activity 5 Complete the conversations below by writing about yourself in the balloons. Then practice using the conversation on the CD.

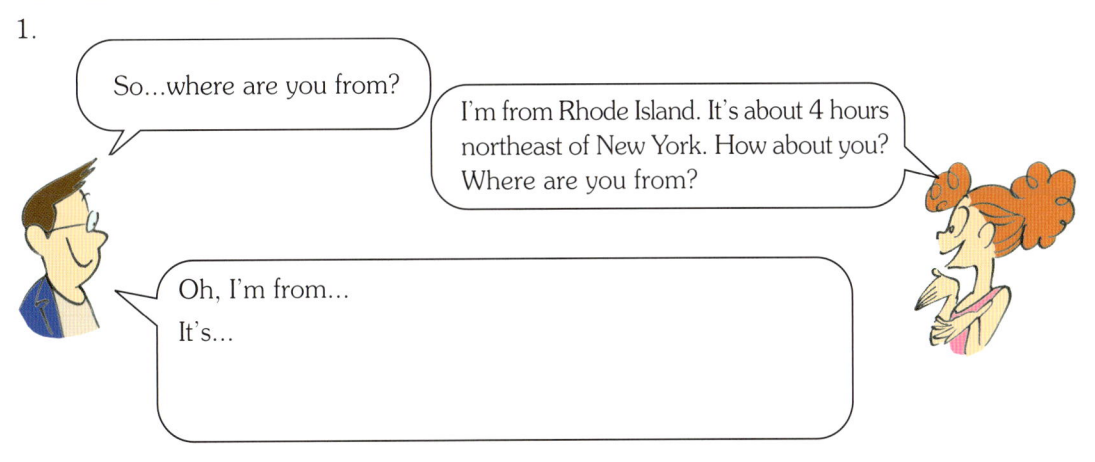

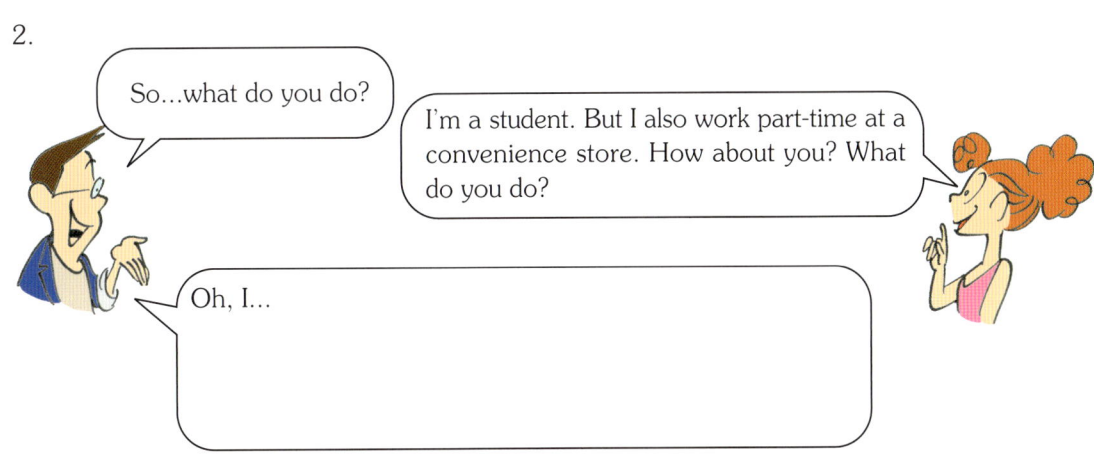

1.

So...where are you from?

I'm from Rhode Island. It's about 4 hours northeast of New York. How about you? Where are you from?

Oh, I'm from...
It's...

2.

So...what do you do?

I'm a student. But I also work part-time at a convenience store. How about you? What do you do?

Oh, I...

Activity 6 Work with a partner. Take turns asking and talking about where you are from and what you do. Extend your conversation by asking questions and making comments.

会話を少ししてから、自己紹介に入ることもできます。

By the way, my name is Mark. Nice to meet you.

Hi, Mark. I'm...
Nice to meet you, too.

Putting It All Together

[1] The Northern Lights
オーロラ

Role Play: Where are you heading?

あなたは日本からカナダ行きの飛行機に乗っています。下の役を交互に、Situation 1 and 2 をパートナーと練習しましょう。

<u>Japanese traveler</u>: 隣の乗客と会話を始め、下の計画から少なくとも2つを選び、旅行の計画について話をしましょう。仕事やその他の個人情報についても話しましょう。

<u>Foreign traveler</u>: パートナーの旅行計画について質問をしましょう。会話の途中に、自己紹介もしましょう。

Situation 1		Situation 2
Japanese traveler's plans		
• study English in Victoria	**100%**	• stay with a friend in Vancouver
• rent a car and travel around	**75%**	• do a lot of shopping
• go skiing with a friend	**50%**	• go camping
• see the Northern Lights[1] (but very far and very expensive)	**25%**	• go to the United States for a day (but need a visa)
	0%	
Foreign traveler		
• You are Canadian.		• You are Australian.
• You are from White Rock (about 40 minutes south of Vancouver).		• You are from Wollongong (about 50 minutes south of Sydney).
• You work as a high school English teacher in Shikoku.		• You are a photographer. You are going to work for a week in Vancouver.

Challenge Role Play: Why don't we go sightseeing together?

Role Play をもう一回練習しましょう。ただし、今回は、一緒に観光するように、計画しましょう。連絡先を交換し、いつ会えばいいか決めましょう。

14　Encounters Abroad

Self-Assessment

Self Assessment Role Play: Over to you!

パートナーと練習してください。このユニットで学んだ内容をもとに、旅行途中の外国人との初対面、という設定でオリジナルロールプレーを作成しましょう。もしクラスあるいは先生の前でロールプレーをする場合、あなたはどこで、何をしているかなどを必ず説明してください。

下のリストを使い、ロールプレーの自己評価をしてみましょう。上手にできましたか。このユニットで学んだ英語をスムーズに、そして正確に使える自信がつくまで、繰り返し練習しましょう。

Meeting People en Route

- ☐ 初対面の人と会話を始めることができる。
- ☐ 他人の旅行の計画について尋ねることができる。
- ☐ 自分の旅行の計画について話すことができる。
- ☐ 他人の旅行の計画について質問をし、コメントやアドバイスも言える。
- ☐ 個人情報について尋ねる/話すことができる。

Language Focus

- ☐ going to や planning to を使い、予定について尋ねることができる。
- ☐ going to / probably / might / want to, but などを使い確実度を表現できる。
- ☐ 旅行の予定だけではなく、週末、夏、その他の計画を表現するため、このユニットの language focus が使える。

Vocabulary

次の単語や表現を使える、発音することができる：

- ☐ I hope
- ☐ Where else…?
- ☐ to head to
- ☐ airline
- ☐ a major
- ☐ Then, after that…
- ☐ rough
- ☐ How long…?
- ☐ actually
- ☐ downtown

2 May I See Your Passport?

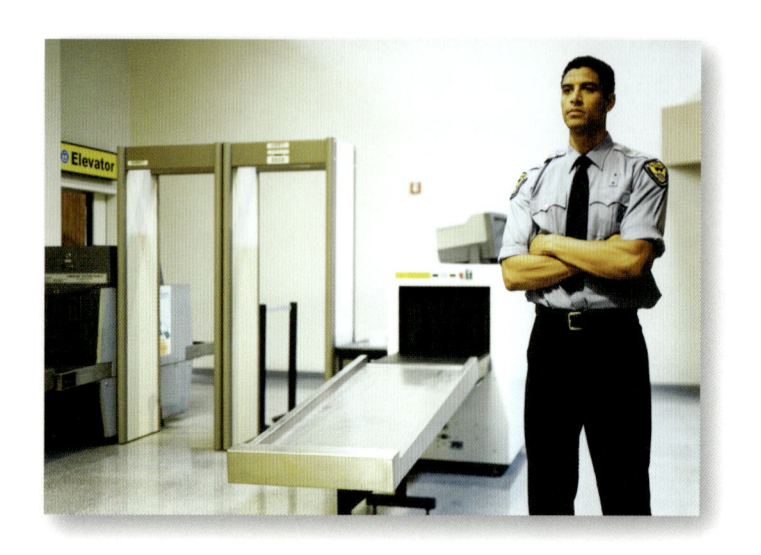

Have you ever traveled to another country?

What country would you like to visit the most? Why?

What documents[1] do you need to enter a foreign country?

海外での入国審査は、セキュリティの強化によって近頃ますます厳しくなってきています。しかし、用意をきちんとしておけば、入国審査では、問題が起らないでしょう。このユニットでは、入国書類の記入や、入国審査で聞かれる質問に答える練習をします。

Warm Up...

Maiは、Canadaに到着し、入国手続きでいくつかの質問に答えなければなりません。会話を聞き、次の質問に答えましょう。

Question 1: 会話を聞き、下の質問を聞いた順番に並べましょう (1 - 3)。

[1] documents 書類

☐ *How long will you be staying in Canada?*

_____

☐ *What do you do in Japan?*

_____

☐ *What is the purpose of your visit?*

_____

Question 2: 上の空欄に各質問の答えを書きましょう。

16 Encounters Abroad

Model Conversation

Going through immigration [1]

Mieko がカナダに到着し、入国審査官と話しています。旅行の計画や、日本での生活、そして荷物についても審査官の質問に答えなければなりません。

Activity 1 Read the conversation with a partner. Write a summary of Mieko's travel information.

Officer: Next. Good morning. May I see[2] your passport and landing card,[3] please?
Mieko: Yes, here they are.[4]
Officer: Thank you. And what is the purpose[5] of your visit to Canada?
Mieko: I'm here to study English and to do some sightseeing.
Officer: And how long will you be staying in Canada?
Mieko: Two months.
Officer: And where will you be staying?
Mieko: I'll be staying with a Canadian family.
Officer: Could you tell me[6] their address, please?
Mieko: Yes. It's the Richmond family. They live at 4694 Haslam Street.
Officer: Thank you. And may I see your return ticket[7] to Japan, please?
Mieko: I'm sorry, what was that?
Officer: Your return ticket. Could you show it to me, please?
Mieko: Oh, yes, of course. Here it is.
Officer: Thank you. And what do you do in Japan, ma'am?[8]
Mieko: I'm a university student.
Officer: I see. And are you carrying[9] any restricted items?[10]
Mieko: No, sir. But I have a few packages of instant noodles. Is that OK?
Officer: That's no problem. Please show your landing card to the customs[11] officer on your way out. Welcome to Canada.
Meiko: Thank you.

---

[1] immigration 入国管理
[2] May I see? 見ていいですか。
[3] landing card 入国審査用の到着カード to land = 着陸する
[4] Here it is / Here they are. はい、これです。物を渡す／見せるときに使う表現。Here is... 〜です Here is my landing card はい、到着カードです
[5] a purpose 目的
[6] Could you tell me... 〜を教えて頂けますか
[7] a return ticket 帰りのチケット to return 戻る
[8] Ma'am は、madam の省略形（ma'am は女性に、sir は男性に対しての敬称）
[9] to carry 持つ
[10] a restricted item 持ち込み禁止物
[11] customs 税関

Language Focus

Talking about future plans

未来の予定を表現するには **will be** + **~ing** も使えます。これは入国審査などのかしこまった状況でよく使われます。しかし、友達と具体的な予定について話をするときも使えます。

Where **will** you **be staying**?
(どこで泊まる予定ですか。)

I**'ll be living** with a host family in Oak Bay.
(Oak Bayでホストファミリーと住む予定です。)

Language Exercise 1: （ ）内の言葉を使い、動詞を **will be** + **~ing** の形に変えて疑問文を作りましょう。そして、その質問に対しての答えを書きましょう。例文を参考にしてください。

1. (How many days / you / stay / in Canada)

   Question: How many days will you be staying in Canada?

   You: _____

2. (Where / you and your friends / go to / this weekend)

   Question: _____

   You: _____

3. (What restaurant / you / eat at / tonight)

   Question: _____

   You: _____

4. (you / study English / in England)

   Question: _____

   You: _____

Language Exercise 2: 友人に "**I'm going to Kyushu**" と言われます。**Will be** + **~ing** を使い、その友達に尋ねたい質問を下に書きましょう。そして、パートナーとその質問を尋ね合い、九州の旅について会話を発展させましょう。

1. Where _____

2. How long _____

3. Will _____

4. What _____

5. Where else _____

6. _____

18 Encounters Abroad

Language Focus

Making requests

[1] to move 引っ越しをする

人にお願いしたいときに **can you**（〜してもらえますか）や **could you**（〜して頂けますか）を使いましょう。**Could** は **can** より丁寧な言い方になります。

Making requests	
Can you take me to the airport, please? （空港まで連れていってもらえますか。）	**Could you** show me your return ticket? （帰りのチケットを見せて頂けますか。）
Can you stop the car, please? （ちょっと、車を止めてもらえる？）	**Could you** open this suitcase, please? （この荷物を開けて頂けますか。）

CD 9

Hey, could you help me with my homework?

Sorry, I'd love to help, but I have to work tonight.

Language Exercise 3: 以下の日本語のリクエストを、それぞれの人物はどのように言うでしょうか。英語で、リクエストとそれに対する答えを書きましょう。

1. Request: 入国審査官があなたの日本の住所を尋ねるとき。

    Immigration officer: _____

    You: _____

2. Request: 知らない人に駅までの行き方を尋ねるとき。

    You: _____

    Stranger: _____

3. Request: 友人に来週末の引っ越し[1]の手伝いをお願いするとき。

    You: _____

    Your friend: _____

4. Request: 友人に8時ごろ電話をくれるようお願いするとき。

    You: _____

    Your friend: _____

Language Exercise 4: **Can** や **could** を使い、以下の人々に頼めるリクエストを書きましょう。1はその例文です。

1. To your teacher: *Could you speak more slowly, please?*

2. To your friend: _____

3. To a hotel staff: _____

4. To a waiter: _____

Unit 2

Communication Focus

Filling out landing cards

[1] citizenship 国籍
[2] province 県（カナダ）
　　state 州（アメリカ）
[3] a postal code 郵便番号

外国行きの飛行機では、書類を少なくとも一枚は渡されるでしょう。このようなカードは landing card（到着カード）と言いますが国によって形も名前も変わります。カナダの場合は、次のカードになります。カードを入国審査官にも免税審査官にも見せなければなりません。

Activity 2   Fill out the landing card below. You do not need to complete Part C.

[4] duration 時間／間
[5] a quantity 量
[6] a resident 国民／住民
[7] a signature サイン

名前、誕生日（年／月／日）と国籍。家族と一緒に旅行している場合は、家族全員がこの同じカードを使い、2, 3, 4のスペースで記入します。

日本の住所

到着の詳細や旅行の目的についての質問

禁止物もしくは特別の事情についての質問。この質問に"Yes"の答えをした場合は、入国審査でさらに細かい質問をされるでしょう。

滞在期間の予定や、カナダに持ち込むギフトの価格についての質問。

Part Aで書いた名前のサイン

Customs Declaration Card

Part A – All travellers (living at the same home address)

1. Last name, first name, and initials / Date of birth / Citizenship[1]
2. Last name, first name, and initials / Date of birth / Citizenship
3. Last name, first name, and initials / Date of birth / Citizenship
4. Last name, first name, and initials / Date of birth / Citizenship

Home address – Number, street | Town/city
Province or state[2] | Country | Postal/Zip code[3]

Arriving by: Airline / Flight no.
Purpose of trip: Study / Personal / Business
Arriving from: U.S. only / Other country direct / Other country via the U.S.

I am/we are bringing into Canada: Yes No
- Firearms or other weapons
- Goods related to my/our profession and/or commercial goods, whether or not for resale (e.g., samples, tools, equipment)
- Food (fruits, vegetables, meats, eggs, dairy products), animals, birds, insects, plants, plant parts, soil, living organisms, vaccines
- Articles made or derived from endangered species
- Currency and monetary instruments totalling CAN$10,000 or more

I/we have shipped goods which are not accompanying me/us.
I/we will be visiting a farm or a farm show in Canada within the next 14 days.
I/we have been on a farm in a country other than Canada during the last 14 days.
(If you answered yes, list country/countries)
1 ___ 3 ___
2 ___ 4 ___

Part B – Visitors to Canada
Duration of stay[4] in Canada (days) | Full value of each gift over CAN$60 | Specify quantities[5]: Alcohol / Tobacco

[6] **Part C – Residents of Canada** (Complete in the same order as Part A)
Date left Canada Y-M-D | Value of goods – CAN$ (including gifts, alcohol, & tobacco) | Specify quantities: Alcohol / Tobacco
1, 2, 3, 4

[7] **Part D – Signatures** (age 16 and older)
1 ___ 3 ___
2 ___ 4 ___

20 Encounters Abroad

Communication Focus

Giving specific information

[1] to repeat 繰り返す

入国手続きを行うときに、入国審査官にいろいろな質問をされます。旅行の詳細や計画、個人情報、荷物についての質問などは、答えられるようにしておきましょう。

Activity 3 Read the model conversation on Page 17. Choose four of the questions or requests that the immigration officer makes and write them below. Then write original responses.

1. Immigration: _____
   You: _____

2. Immigration: _____
   You: _____

3. Immigration: _____
   You: _____

4. Immigration: _____
   You: _____

Activity 4 Work with a partner. Your partner will ask you a few immigration questions. Answer the questions *without looking at your book*. Then ask your partner some questions.

CD 10

- May I see your passport and your landing card, please?
- Yes. Here you go.
- Thank you. And what is the purpose of your visit?
- I'm here to visit a friend and to do some sightseeing.

Asking for repetition

先生や学習パートナー、または海外で出会う人の言葉や質問を聞き取れない場合は、もう一度繰り返して言ってもらいましょう。下の表現を参考にしましょう。

Activity 5 Repeat Activity 4. This time, ask for repetition at least two times.

CD 11

- Sorry, could you repeat[1] that, please?
  (すみません。それをもう一度言って頂けますか。)
- Sorry, what was that?
  (すみません。今何と言ったんですか。)

Unit 2 21

Putting It All Together

[1] a luggage inspection
荷物検査

[2] a customs officer
税関検査官

Role Play: May I see your passport, please?

カナダに到着したところで、入国審査を通らなければなりません。下の役を交互に、Situation 1 and 2 をパートナーと練習しましょう。

<u>Japanese traveler</u>: 入国審査官の質問に答えましょう。20頁の到着カードをコピーし、適切に記入してから練習しても構いません。

<u>Immigration officer</u>: 旅行者をインタビューしましょう。

Situation 1: Business trip	**Situation 2**: Study abroad
You...	You...
• are in Toronto for a business trip.	• are in Halifax to study English.
• will be in Toronto for two weeks.	• will be studying for one year.
• work for a Japanese IT company.	• are a student in Japan.
• will be staying at the Marriot Hotel. (address: 525 Bay Street)	• will be living with a homestay family. (address: 2343 Pinecrest Drive)
• have a few bottles of *sake* as presents.	• are carrying some instant noodles.

Challenge Role Play: Could you open this bag, please?

Role Play をもう一回練習しましょう。ただし、今回は、荷物検査[1] をするため、入国審査官は、あなたに税関検査官[2] に続くように指示します。パートナーは、検査官の役もします。検査官は、荷物を開けるよう指示し、荷物の中身や、あなたがカナダに持ち込もうとする物についていろいろな質問をしましょう。

22　Encounters Abroad

Self-Assessment

Self Assessment Role Play: Over to you!

パートナーと練習してください。このユニットで学んだ内容をもとに、入国審査の設定で、オリジナルロールプレーを作成しましょう。もしクラスあるいは先生の前でロールプレーをする場合、どこの国に入国しているか前もって教えましょう。

下のリストを使い、ロールプレーの自己評価をしてみましょう。上手にできましたか。このユニットで学んだ英語をスムーズに、そして正確に使える自信がつくまで、繰り返し練習しましょう。

Going Through Immigration

- ☐ 到着カードを記入できる。
- ☐ 入国審査での依頼をしたり、答えることができる。
- ☐ 旅行の詳細に対する質問を尋ねる／答えることができる。
- ☐ 禁止物に対する質問を答えることができる。
- ☐ 理解できない際、もう一度言ってもらえるように表現できる。

Language Focus

- ☐ will be + ~ing を使い、予定について尋ねることができる。
- ☐ can you や could you を使い、お願い／依頼ができる。
- ☐ 入国するときだけではなく、このユニットの language focus を使い、自分の予定について話すことも、人にお願いすることもできる。

Vocabulary

次の単語や表現を使える、発音することができる：

- ☐ a postal code
- ☐ a purpose
- ☐ ma'am
- ☐ to repeat
- ☐ customs
- ☐ immigration
- ☐ a restricted item
- ☐ a return ticket
- ☐ a landing card
- ☐ May I see…

3 Where To?

How do you signal a taxi abroad?

Who opens the door in a taxi abroad, you or the taxi driver?

How much should you tip a taxi driver?

タクシーに乗るのは便利なだけでなく、マンツーマンの会話の練習のいい機会にもなります。このユニットでは、タクシーに乗るときに、目的地を言い、運転手と世間話をする練習をします。

Warm Up...

Maiはちょうど空港から出て、タクシーに乗り、ホテルに行く途中です。Maiとタクシーの運転手の話を聞き、次の質問に答えましょう。

[1] St. *Street* の省略形
[2] Ave. *Avenue* の省略形
(Avenue = Street)

Question 1: 運転手が取った道のりを記入しましょう。Maiはホテルに行く途中、タクシーの運転手に一ケ所寄り道するように頼みます。寄り道する場所に丸をつけましょう。

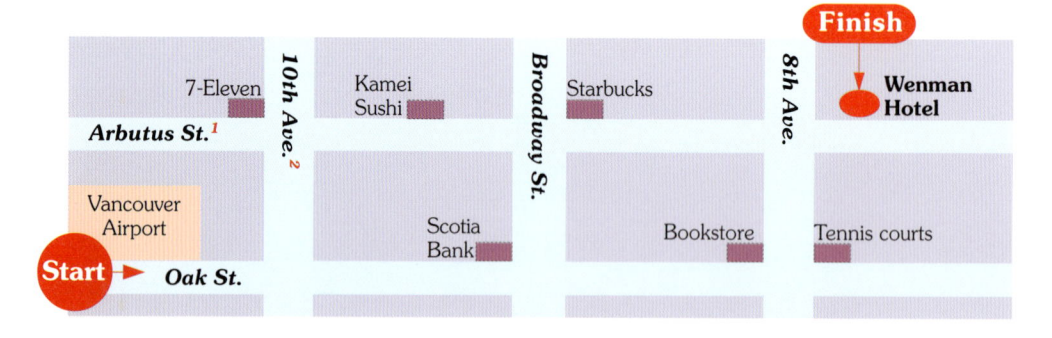

Finish → Wenman Hotel
7-Eleven — Kamei Sushi — Starbucks
Arbutus St.[1]
10th Ave.[2]   Broadway St.   8th Ave.
Vancouver Airport — Scotia Bank — Bookstore — Tennis courts
Start → Oak St.

Question 2: タクシー代と運転手のチップ代をそれぞれチェックしましょう。

| FARE: | ☐ $14.00 | ☐ $24.00 | ☐ $38.00 |
| TIP: | ☐ $6 | ☐ $3 | ☐ $4 |

Model Conversation

Taking a taxi

Kentaroは、空港を出て、タクシーに乗ります。目的地を伝えてから、途中で寄り道するよう運転手に指示します。そしてタクシーの運転手とカジュアルな会話を始めます。

Activity 1 Read the conversation below with a partner. Circle the places Kentaro goes in the taxi, and circle his taxi fare.[1]

[1] a fare 乗車料金
[2] let me... 〜をさせてください
　Let me help = 手伝いをさせてください。
[3] Where to? どちらへ？
[4] ...right? 〜ですよね？
[5] on the way 途中に
[6] to need to... 〜する必要がある
[7] to stop by 寄り道する
[8] on the corner 角で
[9] near... 〜から近く
[10] I'll be right back すぐ戻ってきます。
[11] not/no~ at all ぜんぜん〜ない
　No problem at all ぜんぜん問題ない = どういたしまして
[12] That'll be (price) (値段)になります。
[13] change お釣
　Keep the change とは、お釣は要らないという意味で、チップをあげる時に使う。

Driver: Here. Let me[2] help you with your luggage.
Kentaro: Thanks. Be careful. It's really heavy.
Driver: Wow! No kidding. OK, so...where to?[3]
Kentaro: Could you take me to the Ramada Hotel, please?
Driver: The Ramada? That's the place on Kingsway Street, right?[4]
Kentaro: Yeah, I think so. Oh, and is there a bank on the way?[5] I need to[6] change some money.
Driver: Sure, no problem. I'll stop by[7] the Royal Bank on the way. There's one on the corner,[8] near[9] the hotel.
Kentaro: Thanks.
Driver: So...where are you from?
Kentaro: Japan. I'm just here visiting some friends for a week.
Driver: Oh, yeah. So...what are you planning to do here?
Kentaro: Uhh...I'm going to do some sightseeing, and I'll probably go skiing.
Driver: That sounds like a fun trip. OK, here's the bank.
Kentaro: Thanks. I'll be right back.[10]

Kentaro: Thanks for stopping.
Driver: No problem at all.[11] OK, here's the hotel. That'll be[12] 15 dollars and 25 cents.
Kentaro: Fifteen twenty-five? OK, here's 20 dollars. Keep the change.[13]
Driver: Thanks very much. Actually, let me get your luggage for you. OK, enjoy your trip.
Kentaro: Yeah, thanks. I will. Have a good day.

Language Focus

[1] to clean up　かたづける

Using Let

命令形である **let** は、日本語の「〜させてください」と同じように使われます。左下の列に示されているように、相手のために何かをしてあげたい時は、**let** がいつでも気軽に使える表現です。しかし、右下の列のように、自分のために相手に何かをさせようとする場合は、**let** は多少強いニュアンスを持ち、場合によっては失礼にもなるので、注意して使うほうがよいでしょう。

Using "let"	
Let me take your luggage for you. （荷物を運ばせてください。　＝荷物を持ちましょうか。）	**Let me** see the address. （住所を見せてください。）
Let us drive you to the airport. （空港まで送らせてください。　＝送りましょうか。）	**Let us** use your computer. （パソコンを私達に使わせてください。）

くだけた会話で、**let** はよく使われます。今日の授業で、この隣にある表現を最低一回ずつ使ってみましょう。

Let me try.（私にやらせてよ。）

Let me do it.（私に（その仕事等を）させてください。）

Let me know.（教えて（知らせて）ください。）

Let me see.（見せてください。）

Language Exercise 1: 次の状況と合わせ、**let** を含む文を書きましょう。

1. 友達が新しいパスポートを作った。それを見せて欲しい。
   _____

2. アメリカの友人は、日本語の試験があります。試験勉強を手伝ってあげようと伝えましょう。
   _____

3. 友達と食事をした時、あなたがごちそうしたい。「私に払わせてください」と言いましょう。
   _____

4. 友人が明日日本にくる予定です。何時に到着するかを教えて欲しい。
   _____

5. バイト先で、お客さんが飲み物をこぼした。かたづけ[1]ますとお客さんに伝えましょう。
   _____

Language Exercise 2: 友達と話すときに使えそうな、**let** を含む文を2つ書きましょう。

Language Focus

Talking about prices

下は、米国とカナダの通貨の例です。1 dollar[1] ($1) = 100 cents (100¢) を覚えましょう。

[1] dollar カジュアルな会話では、dollar のかわりに **buck** という言葉がよく使われる。

[2] to come to...（値段の合計が）〜になります
How much does it come to? いくらになりますか。

$1 "looney" $2 "tooney"

海外でも、日本でも、取り引きをするとき、値段について話す必要があるでしょう。

Language Exercise 3: 次の値段を書きましょう。

1. $42.55   _Forty two dollars and fifty five cents_
2. ¥22,402   _____
3. $324   _____
4. ¥348,000 _____
5. $6225.33 _____

Language Exercise 4: 別紙に値段を書きましょう。そして、その別紙を相手に渡し、下の会話のように、その値段について話しましょう。

So...how much does that come to?[2]

OK, here's $70.

That'll be $64.50, please.

Communication Focus

Giving directions to a taxi driver

決まった目的地までの指示は、次の表現を使いましょう。

Stating specific destinations	
Could you take me to the Park Hotel, please? (Park Hotel に連れていって頂けますか。)	That's on Powell Street, right? (それは、Powell Street にありますね。)
I'd like to go to 1663 6th Avenue, please. (1663 6th Avenue に行きたいのですが。)	Sure, no problem. (はい、わかりました。)

[1] Is there a... 〜がありますか。
[2] aspirin バファリンなどの痛み止めを、一般的にアスピリンという。
[3] to change money 両替する I need to change some money お金を両替する必要がある。
[4] to use the washroom トイレを使う

Activity 2 Work with a partner. One partner plays the taxi driver. Be sure to offer to help with luggage and ask, "**Where to?**" The other partner will give directions to one of the following places.

Chateau Victoria Hotel and Suites
740 Burdett Avenue
Victoria, BC
Tel: (250) 382-4221
www.chateauvictoria.com

SAINT MARY'S UNIVERSITY SINCE 1802
923 Robie Street, Halifax, Nova Scotia
Denis Leclaire
Director of International Activities
http://www.smu.ca   international@smu.ca

目的地への途中で、どこかに寄りたい時もあるでしょう。この場合は、どういう場所に連れていって欲しいか、なぜその場所に行きたいか、簡単に説明しましょう。

Is there a[1] drug store near here? I want to buy some aspirin.[2]

Is there a bank on the way? I need to change some money.[3]

Activity 3 Fill in the blanks below. Then repeat Activity 2. This time, ask the driver to stop on the way at one of the places below.

Is there a Starbucks near here?
_____ .

Is there _____ ?
I need to use the washroom.[4]

28 Encounters Abroad

Communication Focus

Chatting with a taxi driver

タクシーに乗っている間、運転手がお客さんと会話を始めようとすることがよくあります。これは、出身、仕事、勉強、旅行の計画などの話をする良い機会になるでしょう。

Activity 4 Work with a partner. One partner plays the taxi driver and asks, "**So...where are you from?**" Develop the conversation for *at least* 5 minutes.

So...where are you from?

Paying the fare

目的地に着くと、代金を払い、チップも適切に払わなければなりません。

Activity 5 Complete each conversation using expressions from the box below. Then read and practice the conversations with a partner.

CD 15

1. Driver: OK, here's your hotel.
   Kana: Great. _____?
   Driver: _____ $16.25, please.
   Kana: $16.25? OK. Here's $20. Thanks very much.
   Driver: Here, _____ with your luggage.
   Kana: Thanks.
   Driver: No problem, ma'am. _____ .
   Kana: I will, thanks. Have a good day.

CD 16

2. Driver: OK, here's the disco.
   Kazuo: Great. _____?
   Driver: _____ $22.45, please.
   Kazuo: $22.45? OK. Here's $26. _____ .
   Driver: Thank you, sir. _____ .
   Kazuo: Yeah, I will. Thanks very much. Have a good night.

have a good time tonight	keep the change	that'll be
how much does that come to		enjoy your stay
that comes to	how much is it	let me help you

Unit 3 29

Putting It All Together

Role Play: Where to?

タクシーに乗ります。下の役を交互に、Situation 1 and 2をパートナーと練習しましょう。

<u>Passenger</u>: 空港から出たところで、重い荷物が2個あります。タクシーを捕まえ、目的地を言い、寄り道をしてもらい、運転手と短い会話をしましょう。

<u>Driver</u>: 欄の一番下には、on the way（向かう途中）の場所と最終的な値段が書いてあります。いいチップをもらえるように、お客さんの荷物を運びましょう！

Situation 1	Situation 2
Passenger	
You want to go to your hotel. You need to stop at a bank on the way.	You want to go to your English school. You want to stop and buy a coffee on the way.
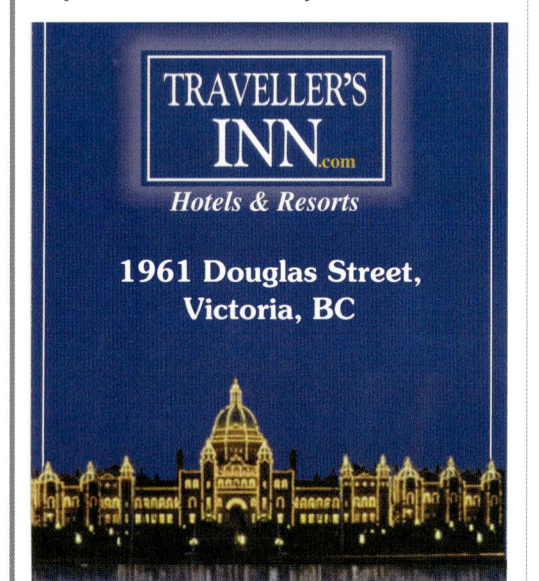 TRAVELLER'S INN.com — Hotels & Resorts — 1961 Douglas Street, Victoria, BC	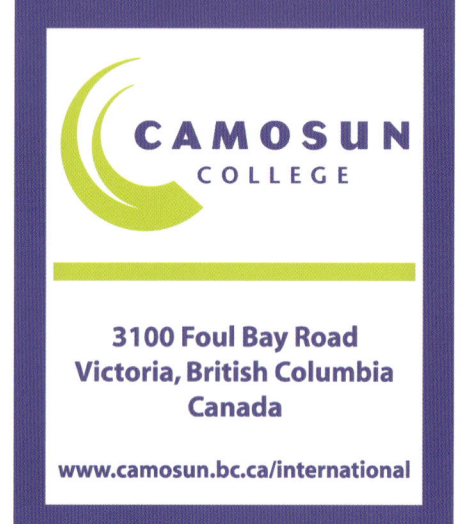 CAMOSUN COLLEGE — 3100 Foul Bay Road, Victoria, British Columbia, Canada — www.camosun.bc.ca/international
Driver	
On the way: Stop at the Royal Bank on Fort Street. **Fare**: $41.25	**On the way**: Stop at the Starbucks on Quadra Street. **Fare**: $24.85

Challenge Role Play: What? This isn't my hotel!

上のSituation 1をもう一回練習しましょう。ただし、今回は、運転手が間違って違うホテルまで行ってしまいます。このミスを運転手に伝え、あなたのホテルに着くよう指示を言います。ホテルに着くと、運転手が違ったホテルまでの分も請求します。間違ったホテルまでの分を払わないように、運転手と交渉しましょう。

30 Encounters Abroad

Self-Assessment

Self Assessment Role Play: Over to you!

パートナーと練習してください。このユニットで学んだ内容をもとに、タクシーに乗る設定で、オリジナルロールプレーを作成しましょう。もしクラスあるいは先生の前でロールプレーをする場合、そのロールプレーの設定を必ず説明してください。

下のリストを使い、ロールプレーの自己評価をしてみましょう。上手にできましたか。このユニットで学んだ英語をスムーズに、そして正確に使える自信がつくまで、繰り返し練習しましょう。

Taking a Taxi

- ☐ 荷物を運ぶ手伝いを申し出ることができる。
- ☐ 運転手に目的地を言い、確認することができる。
- ☐ 途中で寄り道するように指示することができる。
- ☐ 運転手と旅行の計画や個人情報について話すことができる。
- ☐ 支払いし、チップを適切にあげることができる。

Language Focus

- ☐ let を使い、手伝いを申し出る、またはお願いすることができる。
- ☐ 値段を伝えることができる。
- ☐ タクシーに乗る時だけではなく、日常の生活でも let を使える。

Vocabulary

次の単語や表現を使える、発音することができる:

- ☐ Where to?
- ☐ on the way
- ☐ I'll be right back.
- ☐ near
- ☐ that comes to…
- ☐ a buck
- ☐ a cent
- ☐ Keep the change.
- ☐ on the corner
- ☐ a fare

4 I Asked for a Double

Do you sometimes stay at hotels in Japan?

Have you ever reserved a room on the Internet?

Have you ever had a problem when checking into a hotel? What was the problem?

ツアー会社に頼まず、自分で旅行を計画する人が多くなっています。このユニットでは、インターネットでホテルの予約をし、チェックインするときにいろいろな問題を解決し、ホテルの施設について尋ねる練習をします。

Warm Up... カナダに行く前に、Maiはインターネットを使ってホテルを予約しました。そして、今ホテルにチェックインするところです。会話を聞き、次の質問に答えましょう。

CD 17

Question 1: 下に表示されているホテルのパソコン画面の間違いを訂正しましょう。

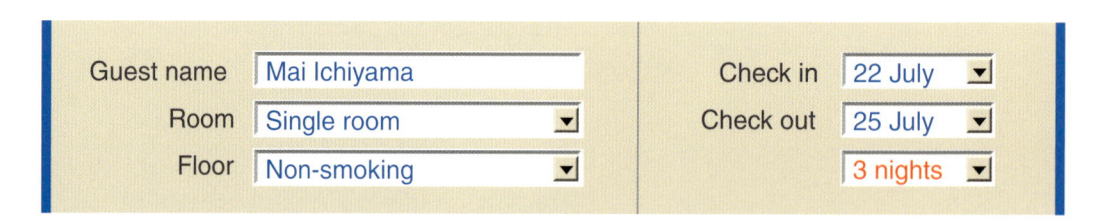

Guest name	Mai Ichiyama	Check in	22 July
Room	Single room	Check out	25 July
Floor	Non-smoking		3 nights

Question 2: Maiがホテルの施設について尋ねます。その情報を記入しましょう。

Fitness center: On the _____ floor, beside the _____

Open from: 7:30 AM to _____ PM   **Cost:** _____

Must have: _____

Model Conversation

Checking in

Azusaは、インターネットで予約したホテルにチェックインします。フロントスタッフがAzusaに挨拶し、予約情報を確認します。それから、支払いやその他の詳細について話します。

Activity 1   Read the conversation below with a partner. Write a short summary of Azusa's hotel details.

CD 18

Reception: Good morning. How can I help you?

Azusa: Hi. I have a reservation[1] for Azusa Hiruma.

Reception: Let me check. Oh, yes, Ms. Hiruma. We have you booked[2] in a double room on a smoking floor, as you requested.[3]

Azusa: *Smoking*? Umm...actually, I asked for a *non*-smoking room. Here's a copy of my Internet confirmation.[4]

Reception: Oh, I see. I'm sorry about that. I'll change that for you right away.[5] OK, I've put you in a non-smoking room. I'm very sorry about the mix-up.[6]

Azusa: Oh, that's OK. No problem.

Reception: All right,[7] then, Ms. Hiruma, could you fill out[8] and sign[9] this check-in card, please? And I'll need to see a credit card, too, please.

Azusa: I'm sorry, could you repeat that, please?

Reception: Uhh...your credit card. We usually require[10] a credit card when you check in.

Azusa: Oh, I see. All right. Here's my card.

Reception: Thank you. OK, here's your card back. And here's your key. You're in room 655. The elevator is just over there.[11] And here are your breakfast coupons.[12] Breakfast is served from 5:30 to 9:30 in the restaurant.

Azusa: I'm sorry. Where is the restaurant?

Reception: Oh, it's on the 2nd floor, beside[13] the elevator.

Azusa: Great. Thanks very much. Room 655, right?

Reception: Yes, that's correct, ma'am. Enjoy your stay.

---

[1] a reservation 予約
to reserve 予約する
[2] to book 予約する (to reserve のくだけた言い方)
we have you booked 予約が確認されています
[3] to request 依頼する
as you requested... お客さんが依頼したように~
[4] a confirmation 確認書
to confirm 確認する
[5] right away 今すぐ
[6] a mix-up 勘違いによるミス
[7] All right = OK
[8] to fill out 記入する
[9] to sign サインする
[10] to require ~が要る
[11] just over there すぐそこに (ある)
[12] a coupon 無料券
[13] beside ~の隣

Language Focus

[1] **a room rate** 一泊の部屋代 (海外のホテルでは、一人当たりの値段ではなく、一部屋の値段で計算される)

[2] **on the side** 別で (ソースなどをかけないで、サイドディッシュに持ってきてほしいときに使う表現)

[3] **shipping** 発送料

[4] **extra large** 特に大きい (多い／小さい等)
an extra large piece (of cake) 特に大きい一個 (のケーキ)

Solving problems

宿泊であれパソコン購入であれ、物を買うときには、問題や誤解が起きることがあります。下の表現を使えば、あなたが遭遇するかもしれない様々な問題を伝えることができます。

Pointing out problems
Actually, I asked for a double room. (実は、ダブルの部屋を頼んだのですが。)
I was told that the room rate[1] was $50. (部屋代が一泊$50だと言われたのですが。)
The hotel brochure said that there were non-smoking rooms. (禁煙の部屋もあるとこのホテルのパンフレットに書かれていたのですが。)

Language Exercise 1: 各状況で、問題を伝えるには、どのように言えばいいでしょうか。

1. ホテルのサイトで、ホテル内にスポーツセンターがあると書かれていたのに実はない。
   _____

2. チェックインするとき、4日間を予約したのに、3日間の予約になっていた。
   _____

3. レストランでサラダのdressingを別[2]で注文したのに、かかったまま運ばれてきた。
   _____

4. 発送料[3]は、無料だと言われたのに、テレビショッピングで買ったものが着払いで届いた。
   _____

Language Exercise 2: 他人が起こした問題やミスに対して苦情を言った経験があるでしょうか。その状況を下に書きましょう。そして、その苦情を英語で書きましょう。

Situation	Your complaint

Language Exercise 3: パートナーと練習しましょう。Language Exercise 1 を使い、各問題に対して、問題を伝えましょう。パートナーは謝り、お客さんであるあなたが満足するまで、問題を完全に解決する努力をしましょう。

CD 19

— Actually, I asked for a piece of cake, not ice cream.

— Oh, I'm so sorry, sir. I'll get you your cake right away. And I'll give you an extra large piece.[4]

— Wow! Thanks.

Language Focus

Filling out Internet reservation forms

[1] total 合計
   total nights 宿泊数
   total charge 計算金額
[2] a single room シングルルーム（1人用の部屋）
[3] a double room ダブルルーム（2人用の部屋）
[4] a twin room 2つのシングルベッドが揃っている部屋
[5] JPY 通貨の省略
   JPY Japanese Yen
   USD United States Dollars
   CAD Canadian Dollars
   THB Thai Baht など
[6] a preference お好み
[7] a first name 下の名前
[8] a last name 名字
[9] to re-enter 再入力する
   （メールアドレスが間違っていないかどうかの確認）

ホテルを予約してくれる会社は、インターネットでたくさん探せます。多くの場合、ホテルに直接予約するよりも、オンラインで予約したほうがとても安くなります。オンラインで予約する場合、部屋代はクレジットカードで前払いする必要があります。次の書類は、オンライン予約書の例です。実際には、このページだけではなく、支払い頁を含め数頁に記入する必要があるでしょう。

Language Exercise 4: 次のオンライン予約フォームを記入してください。

HotelClub.com — Delta Hotel & Suites ★★★★

Fast secure access to over 21,000 hotels across 102 countries!

Navigation: Home | Specials | Membership | My Booking | Customer Service | Partners | About Us

- Check in: d/Mo/Yr
- Check out: d/Mo/Yr
- Total nights[1]

Room Selections (Currency: JPY[5])

Number of rooms per night	Room rate	Number of guests	Total
Single[2] - Instant confirmation	10,100		
Double[3] - Instant confirmation	11,373		
Twin[4] - Instant confirmation	11,373		

All rates shown above are **PER ROOM, PER NIGHT** unless stated otherwise, not per person per night.

Smoking preference:[6] ○ No preference   ○ Non-smoking   ○ Smoking

- Guest first name:[7]
- Guest last name:[8]
- Contact E-mail:
- Re-enter E-mail:[9]
- Contact phone:
- Fax:
- City:
- Country:

Continue — http://www.hotelclub.com

Communication Focus

[1] **PAX** ホテル用語で「客の人数」という意味。
[2] **#** この印は、"number"「番号」という意味。
Confirmation # = 確認番号

Confirming your reservation details

チェックインする際には、下のような表現を使ってフロントのスタッフがあなたの予約を確認します。

Good morning. I have a reservation for Ishitani.

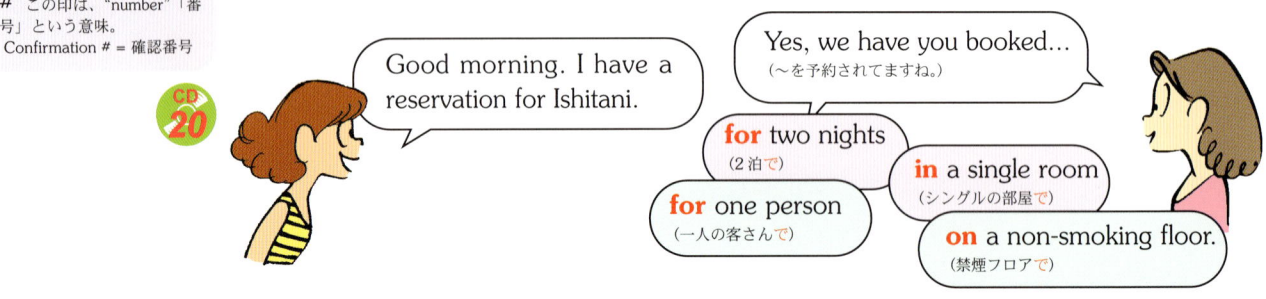

Yes, we have you booked...
(〜を予約されてますね。)

for two nights
(2泊で)

for one person
(一人の客さんで)

in a single room
(シングルの部屋で)

on a non-smoking floor.
(禁煙フロアで)

Activity 2

Below is a hotel computer screen. Write your partner's name in the "**Name**" space, then take turns playing the role of guest and receptionist.

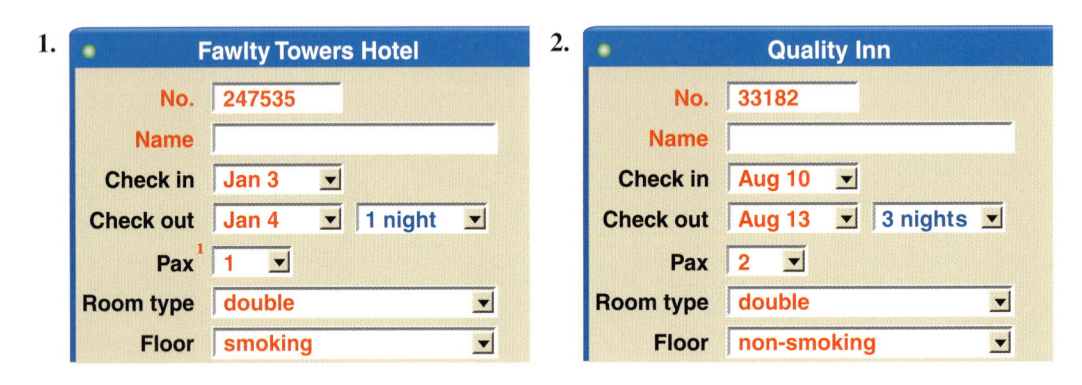

1. Fawlty Towers Hotel

No.	247535
Name	
Check in	Jan 3
Check out	Jan 4 — 1 night
Pax[1]	1
Room type	double
Floor	smoking

2. Quality Inn

No.	33182
Name	
Check in	Aug 10
Check out	Aug 13 — 3 nights
Pax	2
Room type	double
Floor	non-smoking

インターネットで予約する場合、下のような確認が電子メールで届くはずです。チェックインする際に、もし予約内容にミスがあることに気がついたら、必ず言いましょう。

Activity 3

Repeat Activity 2. This time, the hotel guest will use the confirmation e-mail below.

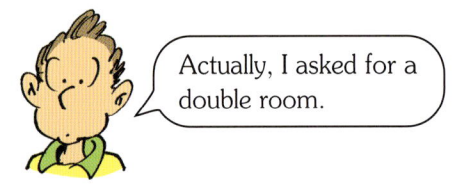

Actually, I asked for a double room.

A double? I'm so sorry. I'll change that right away.

1. From: Fawlty Towers Hotel
Subject: Reservation No. 247535

Confirmation #[2]	247535
Check in	January 3
Check out	January 4 (1 night)
Guests	1
Room type	Double
Floor	Non-smoking

2. From: Quality Inn
Subject: Reservation No. 33182

Confirmation #	33182
Check in	August 10
Check out	August 13 (3 nights)
Guests	2
Room type	Twin
Floor	Non-smoking

Communication Focus

[1] to agree to... 〜をすることを約束する／同意する
[2] an expense 費用
additional expenses 電話代、ルームサービスなど、部屋代以外の費用／雑費
[3] upon 〜する際

CD 21

Completing the check in

ほとんどのホテルでは、チェックアウトする時まで払わなくていいといいながらも、チェックインする際には、クレジットカードを見せるか、現金での保証金を渡す必要があるでしょう。部屋の鍵が渡される前に、チェックインカードに記入する必要もあります。

May I see your credit card, please?

And could you please fill out and sign this check-in card?

Activity 4　Work with a partner. Take turns filling out the check-in card and getting a key.

Arlington Hotel

Guest name: _____　Tel (or e-mail): _____
Address: _____
　　　(No., Street)　　　　　　　　　　　　　　　(City)

　　　(Province / State)　　　　　　　(Country)　　　　　(Postal Code)

I agree to[1] pay the total charge, plus all additional expenses[2] upon[3] checkout.　　Room No.: _1134_
x _____　　　Duty Manager: _J. Pilkington_

OK, here's your room key. You're in room 1134.

Enjoy your stay.

Talking about hotel facilities

チェックインする際、ホテルのレストランやその他の施設について尋ねたい場合があります。

By the way, where is the swimming pool?

It's on the 7th floor. It's beside the gym.

Activity 5　Think of two questions you could ask about hotel facilities. Then work with a partner. Take turns asking and answering each other's questions.

Putting It All Together

Role Play: I asked for a double.

チェックインをします。下の役を交互に、Situation 1 and 2 をパートナーと練習しましょう。

<u>Hotel receptionist</u>: お客さんの予約情報を確認するのに、hotel computer 画面を参照しましょう。そして、黄色のチェックインカードに記入してもらいましょう。

<u>Guest</u>: 下の空欄に、名前を記入してください。そして、下の確認 e-mail を細かく読んだ後、チェックインしましょう。間違いを指摘し、ホテルの施設について尋ねましょう。

	Situation 1	Situation 2
Hotel computer		

Situation 1 — Fawlty Towers Hotel
- Reservation #: A78462
- Guest Name:
- Check in: May 3
- Check out: May 5 / 2 nights
- Pax: 2
- Room type: double / Room 983
- Floor: non-smoking

Guest name: _____
Tel (or e-mail): _____
I agree to pay the total charge, plus all additional expenses upon checkout. x _____

Situation 2 — Quality Inn
- Reservation #: 32456-23
- Guest Name:
- Check in: Dec 15
- Check out: Dec 20 / 5 nights
- Pax: 2
- Room type: twin / Room 1152
- Floor: smoking

Guest name: _____
Tel (or e-mail): _____
I agree to pay the total charge, plus all additional expenses upon checkout. x _____

Guest confirmation e-mail

Situation 1
件名: Re: Reservation: A78462
添付ファイル なし

Dear _____,

Thank you for booking with HotelClub.
Enjoy your stay at Fawlty Towers Hotel.

Checkin: May 3rd
Checkout: May 6th (3 nights)
Guests: 2
Room type: Double
Floor: Non-smoking

Room rate: $125.75 / night

Kindest regards,
Ted McGurk
Bookings office

Situation 2
件名: Reservation 32456-23
添付ファイル なし

Dear _____,

Thank you for choosing Quality Inn.
We look forward to serving you.

Checkin: December 15
Checkout: December 20th (5 nights)
Guests: 2
Room type: Twin
Floor: Non-smoking

Room rate: $78.50 / night

Sincerely,
Scot Kerr
Customer relations manager

Challenge Role Play: I can't stay on a smoking floor!

Role Play をもう一回練習しましょう。ただし今回は、予約したはずの禁煙の部屋はないと言われます。禁煙の部屋は一つありますが、予約した部屋より高いスイートルームです。その部屋をインターネットで予約した部屋と同じ値段で泊まれるように交渉しましょう。

Self-Assessment

Self Assessment Role Play: *Over to you!*

パートナーと練習してください。このユニットで学んだ内容をもとに、ホテルにチェックインする設定で、オリジナルロールプレーを作成しましょう。海外のホテルでも、国内のホテルでも構いません。クラスあるいは先生の前でロールプレーをする場合、どこにいるか、どこのホテルにチェックインしているのかを説明してください。

下のリストを使い、ロールプレーの自己評価をしてみましょう。上手にできましたか。このユニットで学んだ英語をスムーズに、そして正確に使える自信がつくまで、繰り返し練習しましょう。

Checking In

- [ ] インターネット予約用紙を完成させることができる。
- [ ] チェックインする際には、予約情報を確認することができる。
- [ ] チェックインする際に起こった問題を解決できる。
- [ ] チェックインカードを記入できる。
- [ ] ホテルの施設について話すことができる。

Language Focus

- [ ] インターネット予約用紙の語彙を理解できる。
- [ ] *I was told* などの表現を使い、チェックインする際の問題を解決できる。
- [ ] チェックインするときだけではなく、買い物をするときやレストランで注文するときなど日常の場面で、このユニットの language focus が使える。

Vocabulary

次の単語や表現を使える、発音することができる：

- [ ] PAX
- [ ] on the side
- [ ] to book
- [ ] a preference
- [ ] a double room
- [ ] I was told that…
- [ ] a reservation
- [ ] to fill out
- [ ] a first name
- [ ] a mix up

5 What Would You Suggest?

Do you like to go sightseeing in the morning or in the afternoon?

What sightseeing spots would you suggest to a foreigner in Japan?

What kinds of things would you like to do abroad?

行ったことがない場所に旅行する場合、観光の計画を立てるには、地元の人に相談するのが一番でしょう。このユニットでは、旅行者の興味に応じて観光のアドバイスを求めたり与えたりする表現を練習します。

Warm Up...

Mai は Vancouver を観光します。ホテルに観光スポットを尋ねます。会話を聞き、次の質問に答えましょう。

[1] an aquarium 水族館

Question 1: 黄色のボックス内の観光アイディアを、日程表に記入しましょう。

Morning	Afternoon	Evening
•	• • •	• •

- go downtown
- visit Stanley Park
- go to a restaurant by the ocean
- visit Granville Island Market
- walk up Robson Street
- see the aquarium [1]

Question 2: 下の質問に答えましょう。

1. What time does Granville Island Market open? _____

2. How much does it cost to see the aquarium? _____

40 Encounters Abroad

Model Conversation

Asking for sightseeing advice

Hiroshiは、数日間Victoria市にいます。Concierge[1]に観光アドバイスを求めます。Conciergeは、まずHiroshiの興味について聞き、そしていくつかの観光アイデアを提供します。

Activity 1 Read the conversation below with a partner. Underline the suggestions the concierge makes.

CD 23

Hiroshi: Hi. I wonder if[2] you can help me?
Concierge: Yes, sir. What can I do for you?
Hiroshi: Yeah, I have two days in Victoria and I want to do some sightseeing. What would you suggest?[3]
Concierge: Well, what kinds of things would you like to do?
Hiroshi: Well, I'd like to see some of the major sights.[4] And I'd like to do some souvenir[5] shopping.
Concierge: OK, then, I'd suggest that you spend your first day downtown. Most of the major sights are there. You could see the Provincial Museum[6] in the morning. It's very good. Then, in the afternoon, you could do your souvenir shopping.
Hiroshi: That sounds great. All right, so...what about[7] the next day?
Concierge: Well, if the weather is nice, you could go whale watching.
Hiroshi: Whale watching? What's that?
Concierge: Oh, it's great. You go out in a boat to see killer whales.[8] It's fantastic.[9]
Hiroshi: Really? How much does it cost?
Concierge: Well, most places charge about $90 to $120 a person.[10]
Hiroshi: Really? Well, that's not so expensive.[11] Yeah, I might do that. Thanks a lot.
Concierge: No problem at all. My pleasure.[12]

---

[1] a concierge コンシェルジュ、お客様担当係
[2] I wonder if... ～かな？
[3] to suggest 勧める
    What would you suggest?
    あなたのお勧めは、なんでしょうか。
[4] the major sights 主な観光スポット
[5] a souvenir お土産
[6] a museum 博物館
    a provincial museum 州立博物館
[7] What about... ～は？
    What about the next day?
    その次の日は？
[8] a killer whale シャチ
[9] fantastic 最高
[10] a person (per person) 一人当たり
[11] not so expensive そんなに高くない
[12] My pleasure. どういたしまして。

Language Focus

Expressing interests

観光アドバイスを求めるときや、友達と計画を立てるとき、あなたがどのように遊びたいかを相手が理解できるように、まず自分の興味を伝えましょう。

1 local　地元の～
2 cuisine　料理（かしこまった表現）
3 to hang out　特別な用事無しで、ある場所で時間をつぶす／長くいる
4 during　途中／～の間
5 One thing...　～の一つは～
One thing I really want to do is...　私が特にやりたいことの一つは、～

Expressing your interests

I'd like to... （～をしたいのですが。） （丁寧語）	try some of the local¹ cuisine.² （地元の料理を試してみたい）	go skiing. （スキーに行きたい）	see some museums. （いくつかの博物館に行ってみたい）
	see some of the major sights. （主な観光スポットを見たい）	go to a professional baseball game. （プロ野球の試合を見に行きたい）	
I want to... （～をしたいし。） （くだけた言い方）	try some hiking. （ハイキングを試してみたい）	do something outdoors. （外で何かをしたい）	go shopping. （買い物をしたい）
	hang out³ in some places where the locals go. （地元の人がよく行くところで時間を過ごしてみたい）		

Language Exercise 1: あなたが興味あることを2つ書きましょう。

I'd really like to...

And I want to...

Language Exercise 2: あなたは、一年間の留学を予定しています。ホストファミリーがいろいろな計画を立てられるよう、自分の興味を電子メールで送らなければなりません。下のメールを完成させ、最下部に署名もしましょう。

件名：Homestay visit
▶ 添付ファイル なし

```
Dear Mr. and Mrs. Stevens,

Yesterday, I was told to write to you about things that I'd
like to do during⁴ my stay. In fact, I have many interests.

First,

Also,

One thing⁵ I really want to do is to



Well, I look forward to seeing you soon.
Take care,
```

Language Focus

[1] crowded 混んでいる
[2] in the evening 夕方に

Making suggestions

I'd suggest that(〜をお勧めします)や **you could**(〜もできるし)を使い、観光のアドバイスを言いましょう。丸一日の計画の場合は **in the morning**(朝に)、**in the afternoon**(午後に)のような表現も必要となるかもしれません。

CD 24

I'd suggest that you go to Tsukiji in the morning.
(朝、築地に行くのをお勧めします。)

Then, after that, you could go to the Edo-Tokyo Museum.
(そして、その後、江戸東京博物館にも行けるし。)

Or you could go shopping at Odaiba.
(もしくは、お台場まで行って、買い物もできます。)

CD 25

Language Exercise 3: 下の表現を使い、次の観光アドバイスを完成させましょう。

Well, _____ I'd suggest that you go shopping _____ , when the shops aren't crowded.[1] _____ , in the afternoon, _____ visit the museum by the train station. Then, _____ , you could go for dinner by the ocean. _____ that you try the seafood place beside the park. It's fantastic! Then, _____ , you could go skiing for the day.

I'd suggest		**in the morning**
	in the evening [2]	
		you could
on your first day	**then**	**on Sunday**

Language Exercise 4: 住んでいる周辺にある観光スポットや、特にユニークなレストランやショップを下に書きましょう。そして、先生のために、パートナーと一緒に一日の観光プランを立てましょう。

1.	3.
2.	4.

Unit 5 43

Communication Focus

Asking for sightseeing suggestions

観光アドバイスを得るためには、まず声をかけましょう。

[1] temple お寺
　shrine 神社
[2] ~and stuff ～など（口語のみ）

I wonder if you can help me?
（ちょっと、教えてもらえるでしょうか？）

Sure. What can I do for you?
（いいですよ。なんでしょうか。）

そして、アドバイスを求めてみてください。

I want to do some sightseeing today.
（今日は、観光したいのですが…）

What would you suggest?
（お勧めは何でしょうか？）

Giving sightseeing suggestions

観光アドバイスをする前に相手の興味について尋ねましょう。

Well, what kinds of things would you like to do?
（どのようなことをしたいですか。）

Well, I'd like to see some temples[1] and stuff.[2] Also, I want to do some shopping.

Activity 2 You are going to visit your partner's hometown. What kinds of things would you like to do there? Write two ideas below.

Your interests
1. *I'd like to...*
2.

相手の興味を知ったら、観光アドバイスをしてみましょう。

Activity 3 Ask about your partner's interests, then give sightseeing advice about your hometown.

Well, in the morning, I'd suggest that you visit the Dazaifu Tenmangu Shrine.

Then, in the afternoon, you could go downtown.

Oh, and I'd suggest you try Hakata ramen.

If you like ramen, you'll love Hakata ramen. （もしラーメンが好きなら、博多ラーメンが大好きになりますよ。）

44 Encounters Abroad

Communication Focus

Asking about sightseeing details

[1] certainly　もちろん（どういたしまして）

観光のアドバイスを言われたら、値段や営業時間、その他の詳細について、追加の質問を尋ねることも必要でしょう。空欄に自分の質問を記入しましょう。

- How much does it cost?
（それは、いくらですか。）
- Is it crowded?
（混みますか。）
- What time does it close?
（何時に閉まりますか。）
- What's it like?
（どういう場所ですか。）

Activity 4　Your partner is a foreign visitor in Japan who wants to do some sightseeing in Tokyo. Suggest some ideas from the chart below. Your partner will ask questions.

CD 27

- Well, in the morning, I'd suggest that you…
- Wow, that sounds great. What time does it open?

- go to Tokyo Tower
- visit the Edo Tokyo Museum
- go shopping in Akihabara
- go to see a *Giants* game
- go shopping in Harajuku
- walk around Shibuya
- go to see Kabuki in Ginza
- visit the Meiji Jingu Shrine

最後には、いつも通りに、お礼を言いましょう。

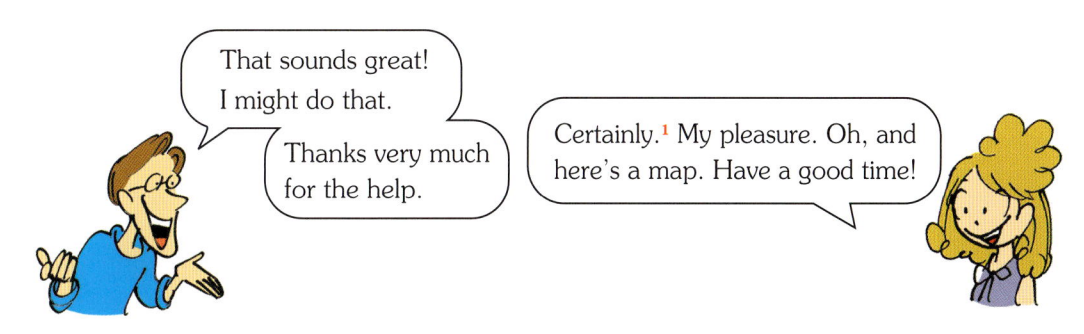

- That sounds great! I might do that.
- Thanks very much for the help.
- Certainly.[1] My pleasure. Oh, and here's a map. Have a good time!

Putting It All Together

Role Play: What would you suggest?

Vancouverでの観光アドバイスが必要です。下の役を交互にパートナーと練習しましょう。

<u>Hotel guest</u>: 観光アドバイスを求めましょう。勧められた場所や行動に対して、追加の質問をしましょう。

<u>Concierge</u>: お客さんの興味を尋ね、それに合わせて下の写真から少なくとも二つのアイデアを勧めましょう。お客さんに質問されたら、想像力を使ってなるべく詳細に答えましょう。

have dinner by the beach
- popular with local people
- can try local cuisine

go whale watching
- costs $95 a person
- boat leaves at 8:30 AM

go shopping on Robson Street
- can buy souvenirs and clothing
- local people often hang out here

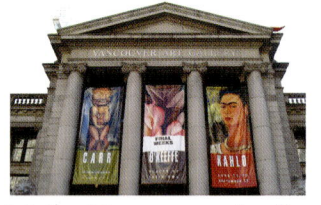

visit the Vancouver art gallery
- costs $15 a person
- open from 10 AM to 9 PM

go to an ice hockey game
- costs $60 to $150 a ticket
- typical Canadian sport

go snowboarding
- about $70 for a one-day lift pass
- very crowded on weekends

Challenge Role Play: Actually, I'm going to Japan in July.

Role Play をもう一回練習しましょう。今回は、conciergeの人があなたに "**Where are you from?**" と尋ねます。答えると、来年の夏にあなたの故郷に行くつもりとconciergeが言い、あなたに観光アドバイスを求めます。Conciergeの興味について尋ね、自分の故郷の面白い観光アドバイスを教えましょう。

Self-Assessment

Self Assessment Role Play: Over to you!

パートナーと練習してください。このユニットで学んだ内容をもとに、観光アドバイスを求めたり、教えたりする設定で、オリジナルロールプレーを作成しましょう。初歩的な準備としては、まず観光場所を決めなければなりません。そしてパートナーに勧められる観光スポットを調べましょう。

下のリストを使い、ロールプレーの自己評価をしてみましょう。上手にできましたか。このユニットで学んだ英語をスムーズに、そして正確に使える自信がつくまで、繰り返し練習しましょう。

Asking for Sightseeing Advice

- [ ] 観光アドバイスを求めることができる。
- [ ] 観光の興味について訪ねたり、述べることができる。
- [ ] 観光スポットや観光プランを勧めることができる。
- [ ] 観光地の詳細について質問することができる。
- [ ] 言われたアドバイスを受け入れることができる。

Language Focus

- [ ] 観光についての興味を表現できる。
- [ ] I'd suggest that や you could を使い、アドバイスが言える。
- [ ] 海外で観光するときだけではなく、国内旅行などのためにも、このユニットの language focus が使える。

Vocabulary

次の単語や表現を使える、発音することができる:

- [ ] sights
- [ ] a souvenir
- [ ] crowded
- [ ] in the evening
- [ ] I wonder if…
- [ ] a concierge
- [ ] cuisine
- [ ] to hang out
- [ ] to suggest
- [ ] not so expensive

Unit Review 1

Extended role play

A trip to Los Angeles

Congratulations on completing Units 1 to 5. 今回のレビューでは、Los Angelesへの旅行をシュミレーションします。今まで習ってきた英語がどの程度使えるか、自己評価になります。

4人組のグループで練習してください。2人は、観光客（**travelers**）の役をし、**全部**のロールプレーをしなければなりません。他の2人は、タクシー運転手など、サポートの役をします。

Travelers
(Students 1 & 2)

Airplane — 飛行機に乗って、隣の乗客と話しましょう。（Students 1 と 2、一緒に）

Immigration — 49頁の landing card を記入し、入国の審査に進みましょう。

Taxi — タクシーに乗り、ホテル The Holiday Inn に行きましょう。

Check in — 49頁にある予約情報やチェックインカードを使い、ホテルにチェックインしましょう。

Sightseeing — Concierge に観光アドバイスを尋ねましょう。49頁の写真を使い、Los Angeles の面白い観光アイディアを勧めましょう。

Landing card

U.S. Department of Justice
Immigration and Naturalization Service
OMB No. 1115-01-03

Welcome to the United States
I-94W Nonimmigrant Visa Waiver Arrival / Departure Form
Instructions

This form must be completed by every nonimmigrant visitor not in possession of a visitor's visa, who is a national of one of the countries enumerated in 8-217. The airline can provide you with the current list of eligible countries.

Type or print legibly with pen in ALL CAPITAL LETTERS. **USE ENGLISH**.

Admission Number
771668572 09

Arrival Record
VISA WAIVER

1. Family Name
2. First (Given) Name
3. Birth Date (day/mo/yr)
4. Country of Citizenship
5. Sex (male or female)
6. Passport Number
7. Airline and Flight Number
8. Country where you live
9. City where you boarded
10. Address while in the United States (Number and Street)
11. City and State

Hotel information

Holiday Inn HOTELS · RESORTS

1020 South Figueroa
Los Angeles, California
Tel: 213-748-1291

Guest Reservation Information

Reservation Number: 45699-23
Guest Name:
Check in: March 10
Check out: March 20   (10 nights)
PAX: 1
Room type: double   (Room# 1268)
Floor: non-smoking

Holiday Inn
Guest Check-In Form

Guest name: _____
Tel (or e-mail): _____

I agree to pay the total charge, plus all additional expenses upon checkout. x _____

Things to do

visit a vineyard
- see how wine is made
- try local wines for free

try bodyboarding
- lessons $40 per hour
- excellent waves

visit Universal Studios
- costs $25 per person
- open until 8PM

go to Beverly Hills
- bus tours cost $25
- tour takes three hours

visit the Getty Museum
- free admission
- beautiful art museum

go watch a baseball game
- LA Dodgers
- $35 per person

Unit Review 1   49

6 Here Are Your Keys

Have you ever rented a car in Japan?

What are the advantages[1] of renting a car? What are the disadvantages?[2]

Which is more important when you rent a car, comfort or price?

北米を旅行すると、公共の鉄道機関が少ないことに気がつくでしょう。町を周るには、車をレンタルしたほうがいいかもしれません。このユニットでは、海外で車をレンタルするとき、どんな車が必要か店員と相談し、レンタルするために必要な書類に記入する練習をします。

Warm Up... Mai は車をレンタルします。会話を聞き、次の質問に答えましょう。

[1] advantages　利点
[2] disadvantages　弱点
[3] economy　経済的／小型
[4] mid-size　中型
[5] full-size　大型

Question 1: Mai はどの車種をレンタルしますか？何人乗りですか？

Number of People	☐ 1	☐ 2	☐ 3	☐ 4
Car Class	☐ Economy[3]		☐ Mid-size[4]	☐ Full-size[5]

Question 2: 一日当たりの値段、期間（何日間）、それから合計の値段を記入しましょう。

Rental Cost	$ _____ / day for _____ days.
	Total Rental Cost: $ _____ .

50　Encounters Abroad

Model Conversation

Renting a car

Hirokiは、車をレンタルしています。使う目的に合った車を選び、レンタル契約書に記入します。最後に、車の傷などを確認するため、店員がHirokiを外に連れていきます。

Activity 1 Read the conversation below with a partner. What kind of car does Hiroki choose?

Hiroki: Good morning. I'd like to rent a car for 4 days, please.

Clerk: All right. And what kind of car do you need, sir?

Hiroki: Well, there are three of us[1] and we all have luggage,[2] so I think we need a mid-size car. What are your rates?

Clerk: Our mid-size cars are $42.85 a day. However, at the moment,[3] our full-size cars are on for[4] only $49.90 a day.

Hiroki: Wow. That's a good deal.[5] Well, in that case,[6] I think that I'll take the full-size car.

Clerk: Great. And do you need insurance?[7] It's $21.50 per day.[8]

Hiroki: Well, it's a little expensive,[9] but, uhh...yeah, OK. I'll take insurance. Thanks.

Clerk: Great. So...with insurance and tax, for 4 days, your rental comes to $352.58.

Hiroki: OK. Here's my credit card.

Clerk: Thank you. And can you fill out this form, please? Oh, and may I see your passport and your international driver's license, please?

Hiroki: Sure. Here you go.[10]

Clerk: Thank you. All right. Let's go outside and check your car.

Clerk: All right, I've checked the car for scratches[11] and dents.[12] Do you see any other damage?

Hiroki: No. It looks fine.

Clerk: OK. Could you sign here, please? Thank you. And here are the keys. Have a nice trip.

Hiroki: Thanks very much.

---

[1] There are ~ of us 私を含めて〜人になる
[2] luggage 荷物
[3] at the moment 今／この時期（かしこまった表現）
[4] to be on for セール金額になっている
[5] a good deal 特に安い値段／良い条件など
[6] in that case それならば〜
[7] insurance 保険
[8] per day 一日当たり 印で書くと「／」を使う。$40/dayは、$40 per day、あるいは、$40 a day と読む。
[9] a little expensive 少し高い
[10] Here you go どうぞ。（物を渡すときに使う）
[11] a scratch 傷
[12] a dent へこみ

Language Focus

Filling out a rental agreement

車をレンタルするときにレンタル契約をする必要があります。内容の勘違いでお金がかかる可能性がありますので、内容を完全に理解した上で記入しましょう。

Language Exercise 1: 下の緑色の注意を読んだ後、書類に記入しましょう。

[1] **if applicable** 必要な場合のみ
[2] **a period** 期間
[3] **an expiry date** 有効期限
[4] **to initial** 頭文字だけでサインする／イニシャルする
[5] **coverage** 保険の範囲に入る条件
   Full coverage = 被害の全額が保険の範囲に入る
[6] **declined** 断られた
   to decline 断る／拒否する
[7] **authorized** 認定された
   to authorize 認定／許可する

Insurance
多少高くても、保険に入ったほうがお勧めです。もし保険を断りたいなら、"Full coverage declined" の箱をチェックし、その隣にイニシャルしなければなりません。

My Pace Rent-a-Car
1547 W. Broadway

RENTAL AGREEMENT

Client Information:

1. Name: _____

2. Address: Company (if applicable):[1] _____

   Street _____ City _____

   Province/State _____ Country _____ Postal Code _____

3. Rental Period:[2] From (dd/mm/yr) _____ To (dd/mm/yr) _____

Passport: Number: _____ Country _____ Expiry Date[3] _____

Insurance:

Please indicate and initial[4] an insurance option. (Please check one only)

- Full coverage:[5] $22.25 / day   ☐
   Accident / loss / damage.

- Full coverage declined[6]   ☐   Renter initials: X _____

Authorized[7] **Drivers**:

Driver 1: _____
Driver 2: _____
Driver 3: _____

I agree that there will be no other drivers except those listed above.   Renter initials: X _____

I have read and agree to the terms of this agreement. If I have presented a credit card for payment, all charges, including photo radar, vehicle impoundment and parking tickets may be charged to the credit card and my signature below will be considered to have been made on the applicable credit card voucher.

Customer signature: X _____

Authorized Drivers:
契約で認定されている運転手意外に運転させると、もし事故を起こしたらあなたは被害額の100%を払わなければならない可能性があります。

Signature
欧米の国では、サインは日本の印鑑と同じように、法律的な結びつきとなります。この書類にサインすると、契約の内容の全てに合意しているという意味になります。この契約の場合は、駐車違法やスピード違反の罰金など、プラスアルファの雑費もあなたのカード会社に勝手に請求する権利をレンタル会社にあげていますので、サインする前に、契約の内容を完全に理解しましょう。

52 Encounters Abroad

Language Focus

Understanding a vehicle ready report

[1] a chip 小さい傷
a crack ひび
[2] windshield フロントガラス
[3] damage free 傷無し
[4] E (empty) ガス欠
[5] F (full) 満タン
[6] passenger side 助手席側
[7] Rep 代表 (Representativeの省略形)

レンタル契約を完成した後、店員があなたを外に連れ、下の用紙を用いて車体の傷などをチェックします。車を返却する際には、もし新しい傷などが見つかったら、レンタル会社はその賠償を請求しますので、注意しましょう。

Language Exercise 2: この書類を使い、家族や知人の車をチェックしましょう。傷を見つけたら、**D** (Dent)、**S** (Scratch) あるいは **C** (Chip/Crack)[1] を記入しましょう。

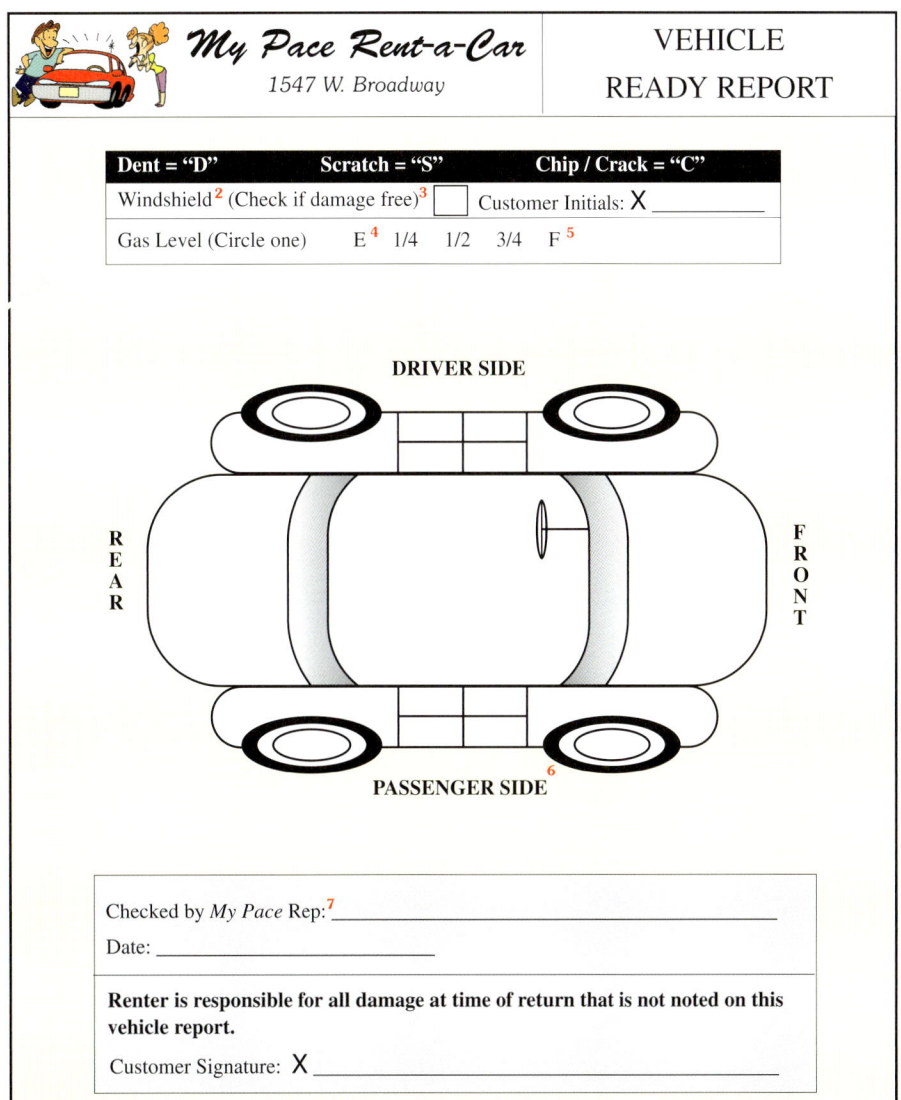

レンタル車を返却する際、レンタル会社から車を借りたときと同じぐらいにガソリンを入れて返却しましょう。もちろんレンタル会社で満タンにしてもらえますが、スタンドで満タンしたほうが圧倒的に安いでしょう。

My Pace Rent-a-Car
1547 W. Broadway

VEHICLE READY REPORT

Dent = "D"　　　Scratch = "S"　　　Chip / Crack = "C"
Windshield[2] (Check if damage free)[3] ☐　Customer Initials: X _____
Gas Level (Circle one)　　E [4]　1/4　1/2　3/4　F [5]

DRIVER SIDE

REAR　　　　　　　　　　　　　　　　　　FRONT

PASSENGER SIDE [6]

Checked by *My Pace* Rep:[7] _____
Date: _____

Renter is responsible for all damage at time of return that is not noted on this vehicle report.
Customer Signature: X _____

他の契約と同じくこの契約は、法律的な書類なので、サインする前に車をしっかりチェックしましょう。

Unit 6　53

Communication Focus

Choosing a rental car

[1] by myself 一人で／自分で
[2] should be... 〜でしょう／と思う An economy car should be OK. Economy型で、OKでしょう。
[3] I don't have much~ 〜を少ししか持っていない
[4] rates （レンタルの）値段
[5] 10% off 1割引き

車をレンタルする際に、店員と相談しながら、economy、mid-size や full-size など車種を決めましょう。

> Hi. I'd like to rent a car for the weekend, please.

> All right. What kind of car do you need?

> Well, I'm by myself,[1] so I think an economy car should be[2] OK.

Activity 2 Imagine that you are going to rent a car. To help plan your rental, check the appropriate boxes below. Then practice choosing a car with a partner.

Passengers	Luggage
☐ I'm by myself.	☐ I have a lot of luggage.
☐ There are _____ of us.	☐ I don't have much[3] luggage.

レンタル会社によっては、平日割引など特別なプロモーションがよくあるので、レンタル代について店員に確認しましょう。

> What are your rates?[4]

> Well, our economy cars are $29.50 a day.
> But this week, our mid-size cars are on for only $39.50 a day.

> Wow! That's a good deal. In that case, I think I'll take the mid-size car.

Activity 3 Take turns renting a car using the information from Activity 2 and the advertisement below.

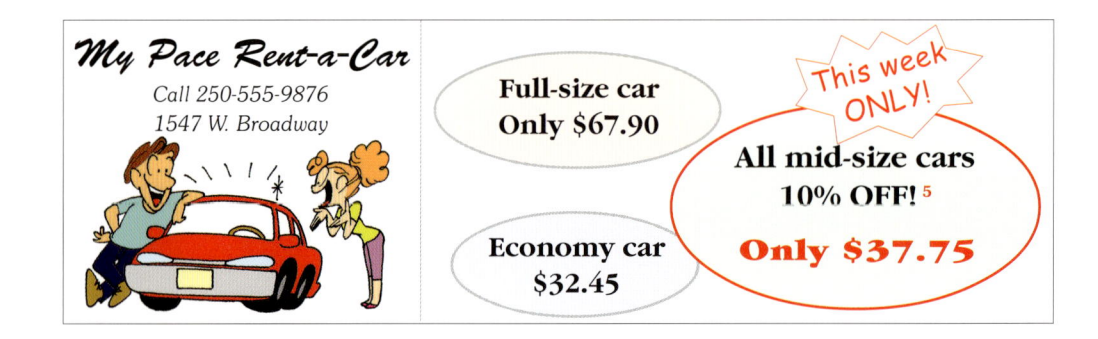

My Pace Rent-a-Car
Call 250-555-9876
1547 W. Broadway

Full-size car Only $67.90

Economy car $32.45

This week ONLY!
All mid-size cars 10% OFF![5]
Only $37.75

Communication Focus

Completing the rental

多少高くても、車をレンタルする際には保険に入ったほうがいいです。

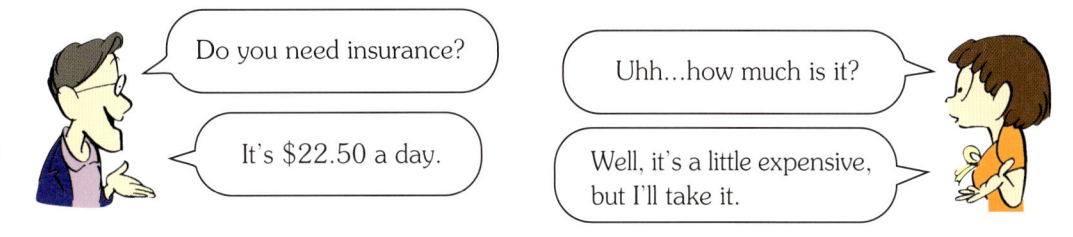

[1] with insurance and tax
保険や消費税を含めて

[2] a form 用紙／書類
（レンタル用の用紙は、52頁を参照）

[3] an invoice 請求書

- Do you need insurance?
- It's $22.50 a day.
- Uhh…how much is it?
- Well, it's a little expensive, but I'll take it.

この時点で、店員がレンタルの合計金額を教えてくれます。車を返却するとき現金で支払うことができますが、レンタルする際には、クレジットカードを見せる必要があります。さらに、国際免許証やパスポートも必要になるので、注意しましょう。

- With insurance and tax,[1] that comes to $188.46.
- Could you fill out this form,[2] please?
- May I see your passport and your international driver's license, please?
- And may I see your credit card, please?

Activity 4 Work with a partner. Use the invoices[3] below. Ask about insurance. Calculate the total rental cost and check the customer's credit card and documents.

1.
   Car class: _Economy_
   Rate: _$33.50_ /day for _5_ days
   ☐ Full coverage: $18.25 / day
   ☐ Full coverage declined

Rental + insurance	$ _____
Tax (14%)	$ _____
Total charge	$ _____

2.
   Car class: _Full-size_
   Rate: _$65.50_ /day for _2_ days
   ☐ Full coverage: $24.75 / day
   ☐ Full coverage declined

Rental + insurance	$ _____
Tax (14%)	$ _____
Total charge	$ _____

Checking the car

最後には、店員と外へ行って、53頁と同じような書類を使い、車体の傷などをチェックします。一旦車をチェックしたら、鍵が渡され、出発です。

- All right. Let's go and check your car.
- Could you sign here, please? Thank you. Here are your keys.

Putting It All Together

Role Play: Here are your keys.

車のレンタルをしています。下の役を交互に、Situation 1 and 2 をパートナーと練習しましょう。

<u>Japanese traveler</u>: ニーズに合わせた車をレンタルしましょう。

<u>Rental clerk</u>: 下の宣伝を使い、お客さんからの値段などに対する質問に答えましょう。52-53頁のレンタル契約や、車準備の書類を使っても構いません。

Situation 1	Situation 2
You are traveling alone. You want to rent a car for ten days. You do not have much luggage.	You are traveling with three friends. You need a car for four days, from Monday to Thursday. You have a lot of luggage.

West Coast Rent-a-Car
604-555-2626
5433 Marine Drive

Mid-size cars
$41.25 / day
Rent more than 6 days
Only $38.50/day!

Economy cars
$32.99 / day

Full-size cars
$59.99 / day
30% off
Monday to Friday!!

Car class: _____
Rate: _____ /day for ____ days
☐ Full coverage: $19 / day
☐ Full coverage declined
Rental + insurance $ _____
Tax (14%) $ _____
Total charge $ _____

Car class: _____
Rate: _____ /day for ____ days
☐ Full coverage: $22 / day
☐ Full coverage declined
Rental + insurance $ _____
Tax (14%) $ _____
Total charge $ _____

Challenge Role Play: I need a new car.

Role Play をもう一回練習しましょう。ただし、今回は、車に乗り、出発してから、エアコンが壊れていることに気づきます。レンタル会社に戻り、違う車を頼みましょう。迷惑の代償として、グレードが一つ上の車などを請求してみてもいいでしょう。

Self-Assessment

Self Assessment Role Play: *Over to you!*

パートナーと練習してください。このユニットで学んだ内容をもとに、車をレンタルする設定で、オリジナルロールプレーを作成しましょう。値段などは、このユニットの中の宣伝を参照してもいいし、自分で宣伝を作っても構いません。

下のリストを使い、ロールプレーの自己評価をしてみましょう。上手にできましたか。このユニットで学んだ英語をスムーズに、そして正確に使える自信がつくまで、繰り返し練習しましょう。

Renting a Car

- ☐ 自分のニーズに合った車を選ぶことができる。
- ☐ 値段について話し合うことができる。
- ☐ 保険に入るかどうかを決めることができる。
- ☐ レンタル契約を記入することができる。
- ☐ 傷などの最終的なチェックができる。

Language Focus

- ☐ レンタル契約を読む、理解することができる。
- ☐ vehicle ready report を読む、理解することができる。
- ☐ decline や signature など、車をレンタルするときだけではなくいろいろな契約で用いられている語彙を理解できる。

Vocabulary

次の単語や表現を使える、発音することができる：

- ☐ in that case
- ☐ if applicable
- ☐ insurance
- ☐ at the moment
- ☐ by myself
- ☐ a scratch
- ☐ mid-size
- ☐ a little expensive
- ☐ luggage
- ☐ per day

7 Turn Left at the Light

Do you ever ask for directions in Japan?

Have you ever given directions to a foreigner in Japan?

After giving a foreigner directions, what things could you ask him or her?

旅行するとき、道を訪ねるのは、大切なことです。そして、英会話を練習する良い機会となり、新しい友人を作るチャンスとなります。このユニットでは、道を尋ねたり、教えたりしながら、外国人とカジュアルな会話ができるように練習します。

Warm Up... Maiはバスステーションを探しています。すれちがう人に道を尋ね、そして、短い会話をします。彼らの会話を聞き、次の質問に答えましょう。

Question 1: MaiとDanielは地図にある **Start** 地点にいます。Danielが教えている道順を記入し、最後には、バスステーションの場所に丸をつけましょう。

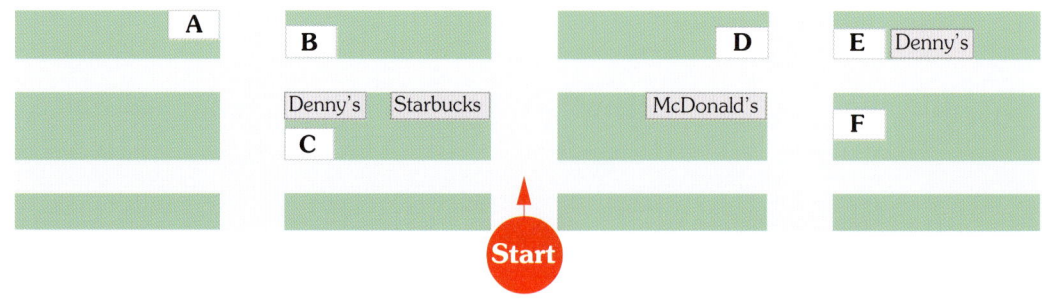

	A		B			D		E	Denny's
		Denny's	Starbucks		McDonald's		F		
			C						

Start

Question 2: 下の質問に答えましょう。

1) Why is Mai going to Port Alberni? _____

2) Why is Daniel living in Vancouver? _____

58 Encounters Abroad

Model Conversation

Asking directions

Akane達は、地元の人(Corey)を道で呼び止め、道を尋ねます。Coreyは、会話が続くように、博物館の話をし、連絡先をAkane達に教えます。

Activity 1

CD 33

Read the conversation below with a partner. Then draw a simple map showing the location of the Provincial Museum.

Akane: Excuse me.

Corey: Yes?

Akane: We're trying to[1] find the Provincial Museum. Could you tell us how to get there?[2]

Corey: Sure. It's easy. Just walk up this street and turn left at the second intersection.[3] You'll see[4] the museum on your left.

Akane: On my left? OK, got it.[5] Thanks very much.

Corey: Sure. No problem. You'll like the museum. It's great.

Akane: Yeah, actually, I've heard it's fantastic. So...are you from Victoria?

Corey: Yeah, I am. How about you? Where are you guys[6] from?

Akane: We're all from Japan.

Corey: Oh, yeah. So...how long will you be staying in Victoria?

Akane: About two weeks. We're planning to do some sightseeing around the city for a few days. Then we'll probably rent a car and travel around a little.

Corey: Cool. Well, I hope you have good weather for your trip.

Akane: Thanks. By the way, my name is Akane. And this is Yoshiko and Atsushi.

Corey: Hi. Nice to meet you guys. I'm Corey. Actually, here's my card.[7] Give me a call if you need any more sightseeing advice.

Akane: Yeah, we might do that. Thanks very much.

Corey: Sure. No problem. Hey, listen, I have to go. I have to get to work. Enjoy the museum.

Akane: Yeah, we will. Thanks, Corey. See ya.[8]

---

[1] trying to... 〜しようとしている We're trying to find 見つけようとしている／探している

[2] to get there そこに着く I got there at 2PM = I arrived at 2PM

[3] intersection 交差点

[4] you'll see 見えてくる you'll see it on your left 左側に見えてきます

[5] Got it 分かりました（くだけた言い方）

[6] you guys あなた達（くだけた表現）

[7] Here's my card 名刺です。

[8] ya youのくだけた言い方 See ya! またね！

Language Focus

Imperative form

[1] There's no place to park 駐車場がない

命令形は、人に指示をするときに使われます。命令形は動詞の原形と同じです。下には肯定文や否定文の命令形の例があります。自分の例を作り、空欄に書きましょう。

Turn left at the intersection.
(交差点で左に曲がってください。)

Don't go to that movie. It's terrible!
(あの映画を見に行かないでください(行かない方がいい)。最悪だからです。)

Language Exercise 1: CDを聞きながら次の空欄を埋めましょう。

CD 34

Foreigner: Excuse me. I need to buy a ticket to Yokohama, but I'm not sure how this machine works. Could you help me?

Masumi: Sure, no problem. OK, uhh...first, _____ Yokohama on the map up here. Let's see. It's 1120 Yen. All right, now _____ some money in the slot here.

Foreigner: OK. Here's 2,000 Yen. I put it in here, right?

Masumi: Ahh...no, _____ it there. That's for pre-paid train cards.

Foreigner: Oh, I see. It goes here, right?

Masumi: Yeah, that's right. OK, now _____ the 1120 button. Then _____ your ticket. And _____ to take your change.

Language Exercise 2: 次の表現を英語にしましょう。

1. Starbucksまで歩いて、左に曲がってください。
   _____

2. 私に電話するのを忘れないでください。
   _____

3. お湯を沸かして、そして味噌をゆっくりと入れてください。
   _____

4. 駐車場がない[1]ので、車で行かないほうがいいです。
   _____

Language Exercise 3: 命令形を使いcup noodleの作り方を説明してください。

Hey, could you show me how to make these cup noodles?

Sure, no problem. It's easy. First,...

60 Encounters Abroad

Language Focus

Direction commands

道案内をするための命令形表現やその他の表現が下の欄にあります。

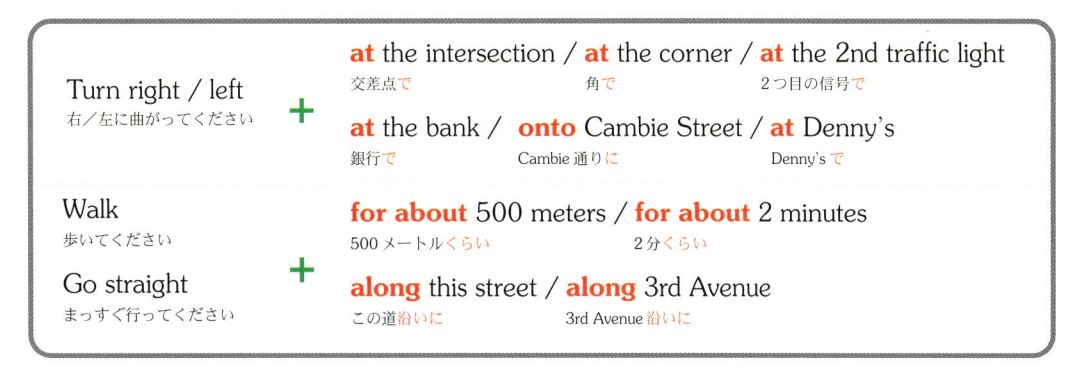

Turn right / left 右／左に曲がってください	**+**	**at** the intersection / **at** the corner / **at** the 2nd traffic light 交差点で　　　　　　　角で　　　　　　　　2つ目の信号で **at** the bank / **onto** Cambie Street / **at** Denny's 銀行で　　　　Cambie 通りに　　　　　Denny's で
Walk 歩いてください	**+**	**for about** 500 meters / **for about** 2 minutes 500メートルくらい　　　　　2分くらい
Go straight まっすぐ行ってください		**along** this street / **along** 3rd Avenue この道沿いに　　　　　3rd Avenue 沿いに

道案内は、いくつかの言い方で表現できます。下の例のように、簡単な右折でも、いろいろな表現で伝えることができます。

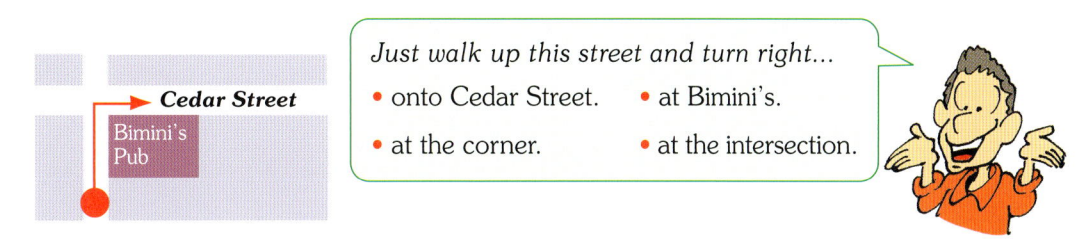

Just walk up this street and turn right...
- onto Cedar Street.
- at Bimini's.
- at the corner.
- at the intersection.

Language Exercise 4: 地図の赤い矢印が示すように、下にある空欄に道案内を書いてください。必要に応じて、**and** や **then** で道案内の表現を接続しましょう。

❶ *Just walk up this street and...*

❷

❸

❹

Unit 7　61

Communication Focus

Getting directions from a stranger

[1] an embassy 大使館

道を訪ねるときに、まず声をかけます。そしてあなたが探している場所までの道を尋ねます。

> Excuse me.
> （すみません。）
> I'm trying to find the museum.
> Could you tell me how to get there?
> （博物館を探しているのですが、そこまでの道を教えて頂けますか。）

61頁のような表現と共に、下に示されている **you'll see** も使いましょう。道案内をより分かりやすくするために、指を差したり、ジェスチャーも使いましょう。

> Go straight and **you'll see** a Denny's on your left.
> （この道をまっすぐ歩くと、Denny'sが左側に見えてきます。）

> Turn left there and **you'll see it** on your right.
> （そこで左にまがると、右側に見えてきます。）

Activity 2

Listen to the three conversations on the CD. Start at the **Start** point below. For each conversation, follow the directions in pencil on the map. Circle the final destination.

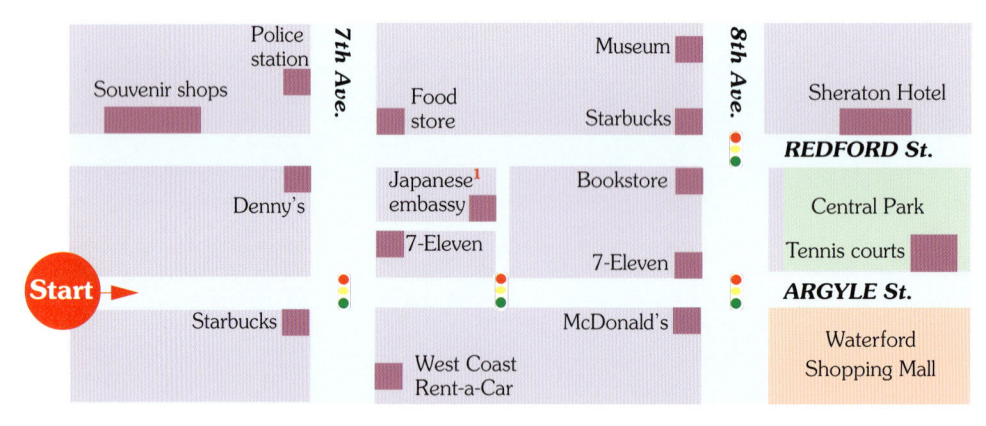

(CD 36 – CD 38)

[Map showing streets: 7th Ave. and 8th Ave. running vertically; REDFORD St. and ARGYLE St. running horizontally. Locations include: Police station, Souvenir shops, Museum, Sheraton Hotel, Food store, Starbucks, Denny's, Japanese embassy[1], Bookstore, Central Park, 7-Eleven, Tennis courts, Start point, Starbucks, McDonald's, West Coast Rent-a-Car, Waterford Shopping Mall.]

Activity 3

Work with a partner. Choose one of the places on the map above and ask for directions. When giving directions, use gestures.

道を教えてもらったら、必ずお礼を言いましょう。

> OK, got it. Thanks very much.
> （はい。わかりました。ありがとうございます。）

62 Encounters Abroad

Communication Focus

Small talk with a stranger

道を教えてもらった後、会話を続けたい場合もあるでしょう。下の例文は、話のきっかけとして使えます。

So...are you from around here?
(この町はあなたの地元ですか。)

So...is this your first time in Canada?
(カナダに来るのは、初めてですか。)

So...how do you like it here?
(ここ (この国／町など) は、どうですか。)

そして、旅行、大学の専攻、仕事についてなど、いろいろな話ができます。下に示されている表現を使い、自己紹介し、連絡先の交換もできます。

By the way, my name is Maria.

Here's my card. Call me if you need any help.

This is my e-mail address. Let me know if you plan to visit Japan.

Activity 4 Work with a partner. Each partner will take an identity below. Using one of the conversation starters above, start and maintain a three-minute conversation, then introduce yourself.

1. **Bushwood**
Golf and Country Club
Trent D. Walsh
Assistant Greenskeeper
Tel: (250) 555-6534
wally@bushwood.com

2. **WORLDTALK**
Language and Communication
3214 W. 4th
Vancouver, BC
604-555-6743
http://www.encounters.jp
Kathy Romas
English Instructor

会話を終えるには、次の表現が使えます。

Listen, I have to go.
(すみませんが行かなければなりません。)

Have a nice trip.
(楽しい旅行を。)

It was nice meeting you.
(お会いできて良かったです。)

Thanks for the help.
(手伝ってくれてありがとう。)

Putting It All Together

[1] Bus terminal　バスターミナル
[2] Parliament buildings　州会議事堂
[3] Wax Museum　ろう人形館

Role Play: Turn left at the light.

道を尋ねます。下の役を交互に、パートナーと練習しましょう。

<u>Japanese traveler</u>: 下の地図で行きたい場所を選び、**Start**地点から道を尋ねましょう。

<u>Foreigner</u>: **Start** 地点から、道を教えましょう。自分の役は、63頁のActivity 4から選んでも、自分の役を作っても構いません。

Challenge Role Play: Sorry, but I don't have e-mail.

Role Playをもう一回練習しましょう。ただし、今回は、道を教えてくれる人が少し変わった人のようです。道を教えた後、あなたの電話番号やメールアドレスを聞いてきます。連絡先を教えないように、上手に会話を終わらせましょう。

64　Encounters Abroad

Self-Assessment

Self Assessment Role Play: Over to you!

パートナーと練習してください。このユニットで学んだ内容をもとに、道を尋ねるとき、外国人と初めて会話する設定で、オリジナルロールプレーを作成しましょう。地図は、このユニットの中の地図でも、自分で作ったオリジナルの地図でも、インターネットで見つけたあなたが行きたい旅行先の地図でも、どれを使っても構いません。

下のリストを使い、ロールプレーの自己評価をしてみましょう。上手にできましたか。このユニットで学んだ英語をスムーズに、そして正確に使える自信がつくまで、繰り返し練習しましょう。

Asking Directions

- ☐ 道を尋ねることができる。
- ☐ 道を教えることができる。
- ☐ 地元の人と会話を始めることができる。
- ☐ 地元の人と会話を続けることができる。
- ☐ 連絡先の交換ができる。

Language Focus

- ☐ 道案内をするために、命令形を使える。
- ☐ 道案内をするのに、いくつかの表現を用いることができる。
- ☐ 道案内をするだけではなく、日常会話の中でカップヌードルの調理の仕方や、その他の説明をするために、命令形が使える。

Vocabulary

次の単語や表現を使える、発音することができる：

- ☐ an intersection
- ☐ a traffic light
- ☐ on your right
- ☐ you guys
- ☐ Got it.
- ☐ at the corner
- ☐ Here's my card.
- ☐ to get (there)
- ☐ along this street
- ☐ go straight

8 How Much Is This?

If you go abroad, what kinds of things will you buy?

What products do you think will be cheaper abroad? What things might be more expensive?

Is it possible to negotiate prices abroad?

海外旅行では、自分のために買い物をしたり、友人や家族のためにお土産を買うことでしょう。このユニットでは、買い物をするときに店員と商品についての会話や、値段について交渉する練習をします。

Warm Up...

Maiは、大きなデパートで靴、お土産などの買い物をしています。店員との会話を聞き、次の質問に答えましょう。

[1] a carving ナイフで彫った小さな像（彫刻）
[2] each 〜ずつ
[3] sales tax 消費税

Question 1: Maiの依頼を完成させるように、正しいボックスにチェックし、空欄を埋めましょう。

1. These shoes are ☐ a little big. / ☐ a little tight.   Can I try a _____ size, please?

2. If I buy _____ carvings,[1] can I get ☐ a more expensive one? / ☐ a better price?

Question 2: お土産の単価を左の表に記入し、消費税と店員が出した会計を右の表に記入しましょう。

Baseball hats:	$ _____ each[2]	**Sales tax**:[3] _____ %
Jade Carvings:	$ _____ each	**TOTAL**: $ _____

66 Encounters Abroad

Model Conversation

Shopping

Kiyomiがお土産店でCowichan sweater[1]を見ています。自分のサイズを見つけるために、店員に手伝ってもらいます。そして、他のお土産も見ます。少しでも安く買えるよう、店員と交渉し、最後に、商品の支払いをします。

Activity 1   Read the conversation below with a partner. Circle the items that Kiyomi decides to buy.

Clerk: Hi. Can I help you?

Kiyomi: Yes. Can I try on[2] this sweater?

Clerk: Of course. How does it fit?[3]

Kiyomi: Actually, it's a bit loose around the shoulders.[4] Do you have a smaller size?[5]

Clerk: Sure, just let me check. All right, here's an extra small. How does it fit?

Kiyomi: Oh, it's perfect. I'll take it.[6] Oh, and I'd like to buy a few souvenirs for my friends. What would you suggest?

Clerk: Well, how about these coffee table books?[7]

Kiyomi: I don't know. They're pretty heavy. Do you have something lighter?

Clerk: Well, we have these wood carvings. They're quite light.

Kiyomi: Wow. They're beautiful! How much are they?

Clerk: They're $50 each.

Kiyomi: $50? That's a little expensive. If I buy four, can you give me a better price?

Clerk: Four? Well, I think I could give you 5% off.

Kiyomi: Really? Great. Thanks. OK, then, I'll take, uhh…these three carvings here, and this one here. And I think that'll be all for today, thanks.

Clerk: OK, so that's[8] the Cowichan sweater and the carvings. With tax, that comes to $409.26, please.

Kiyomi: Can I put it on my credit card?

Clerk: Sure, no problem. Just sign here, please. Great. Thank you very much.

---

[1] a Cowichan sweater カナダの西海岸の原住民が作る伝統的な服。カナダの有名なお土産の一つ。

[2] to try on （洋服を）試してみる

[3] How does it fit? サイズはどうですか。

[4] loose around the shoulders 肩の辺がゆるい

[5] a smaller size より小さいサイズで

[6] I'll take… ～をお願いします
I'll take it これをお願いします
I'll take these これらをお願いします
I'll take one これらの一つをお願いします

[7] a coffee table book 大きな写真入りの本

[8] OK, so that's… では、～になります。

Language Focus

Making specific complaints

買い物をするときに、左下の太字の強意語と右下の形容詞を使い、商品に対しての不満なポイントを具体的に伝えましょう。

[1] around the waist ウエストのあたり
[2] tight きつい
[3] can / can't afford 〜する余裕がある／ない I can't afford to buy it. それを買う余裕がない
[4] I wish I had + 過去分詞 すればよかったのに I wish I had bought it. 買えばよかった。

a little (少し)
a bit (多少)
quite (かなり)
pretty (かなり)
really (とても)
too (〜すぎる)

+

big (large) / small (大きい／小さい)
long / short (長い／短い)
dark / light (濃い色／明るい)
heavy / light (重い／軽い)
expensive / cheap (高い／安い)
tight / loose (きつい／緩い)

So...how does everything fit?

Well, the jeans are **a little loose** around the waist,[1] and **too long**. And this shirt is **quite tight**[2] around the neck.

Language Exercise 1: 強意語と形容詞を使い、下の会話を完成させましょう。

1. Clerk: So...how do those jeans fit?
   You: Well, they're _____ , but I really like the style. I'll take them.

2. You: Sorry, but this one is _____ . I can't afford[3] it.
   Clerk: All right. Well, how about this model? It's much cheaper, but it's still very good.

3. You: These shoes are _____ . Could I try a half-size smaller?
   Clerk: Sure, no problem. Try these ones on. They're a size 9.

4. Friend: Hey, I heard you bought a video camera on the Internet. How is it?
   You: Oh, it's pretty good. But it's _____ . I wish I'd[4] bought one that weighs a little less. But it was _____ , so even if it's not perfect, I'm happy about the price.

Language Exercise 2: 下の例文で示されているように、空欄に不満な点の例を書きましょう。

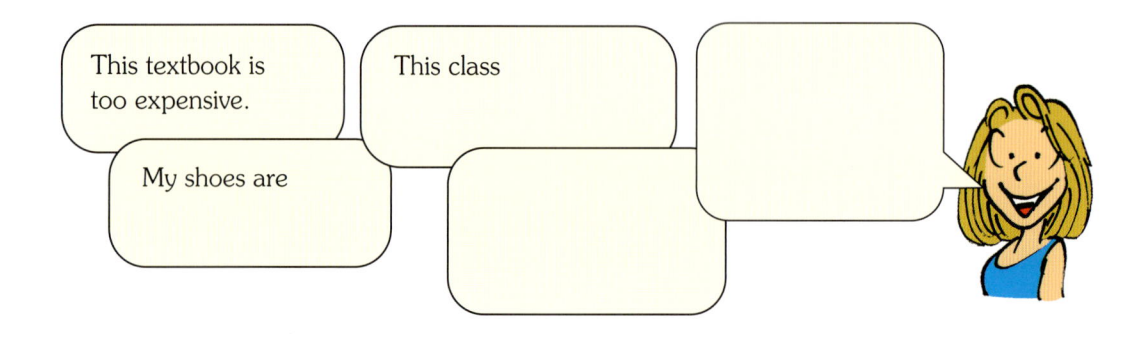

This textbook is too expensive.

This class

My shoes are

Language Focus

[1] Do you have… …がありますか。
[2] to agree 賛成
[3] to disagree 反対
[4] intelligent 知的／頭のいい

Making comparisons

カジュアルな会話では比較級がよく使われます。比較級の作り方のルールは単語の音節の数によって決まります。

ほとんどの1や2音節の形容詞 + **er (than)**: cheap → cheap**er**　funny → funn**ier** （安い）　（より安い）　（面白い）　（より面白い）	Do you have a cheap**er** one? （より安いものがありますか。） Japanese movies are funn**ier than** American ones. （日本の映画は、アメリカの映画よりもユーモアがある。）
more / less + 3音節以上の形容詞 **(than)**: expensive → more / less expensive （高い）　（より高い／より高くない）	Can I see a **less** expensive brand? （これより高くないブランドを見せてもらえますか。） iPODs are **more** popular **than** other MP3 players. （iPODは他のMP3プレーヤーより人気がある。）
例外もあります。 good / bad → **better / worse** （良い）（悪い）　（より良い）（より悪い） fun → **more fun** （楽しい）　（より楽しい）	Can you give me a **better** price? （もう少し安い値段にできますか。） Being with a friend is **more** fun **than** being alone. （友達と一緒にいるのは、一人でいるより楽しい。）

Language Exercise 3: ( ) 内の形容詞の比較級を空欄に書き、次の文章を完成させましょう。

1. This souvenir is quite big. Do you have[1] a (small) _____ one?

2. This hotel is much (good) _____ than the other hotel. I like it.

3. These shirts are too dark. Do you have any in a (light) _____ color?

4. This is really expensive. Do you have a (expensive) _____ one?

5. I like this, but do you have one that's a little (cheap) _____ ?

6. These shoes are a bit too tight. Can I try a (large) _____ size, please?

Language Exercise 4: 次の発言を **agree** か **disagree** でチェックしましょう。自分の意見をパートナーとディスカッションしましょう。

	I agree[2]	I disagree[3]
1. *McDonald's* is better than *Mos Burger*.	☐	☐
2. Studying English is more useful than studying math.	☐	☐
3. Eating pizza is healthier than eating cup noodles.	☐	☐
4. Women are more intelligent[4] than men.	☐	☐
5. Love is less important than money.	☐	☐

Communication Focus

Shopping

買い物をする際、値段を尋ねたり、洋服を試していいかどうか、店員に尋ねる場合があります。

[1] Can I... 〜していい？

Hi. Can I help you?
(何かお探しですか。)

Yes. How much is this (are these)?
(はい。これ（これら）は、いくらですか。)

Yes. Can I[1] try this on?
(これを着てみていいですか。)

必要に応じて、商品に対して不満を言い、代わりの商品を頼みましょう。

Do you have any darker ones?
(これより色が濃いのがありますか。)

Yes. How about this one?
(はい、この商品は、どうですか。)

This is great. **I'll take it.**
(これは、ちょうどいいですね。これをお願いします。)

Activity 2

Write a specific complaint about each item below. Then work with a partner and practice shopping for those items.

This watch _____
_____ .

Do you have a less expensive model?

$189

$49.99

靴や洋服を買うときに、次の表現が役に立つでしょう。

How does it fit?
(サイズのほうは、どうですか。)

It's perfect. I love it.
(ちょうどいいです。気に入りました。)

It looks great on you.
(よくお似合いですよ。)

How does it look?
(似合いますか。)

Activity 3

Take turns buying shoes and a jacket. Use your own clothing as the items you buy.

Excuse me. Do you have these shoes in a larger size?

Communication Focus

Negotiation and payment

一つの店でたくさん買うなら少し値下げを、あるいは無料でグッズをもらえるよう、交渉してみましょう。必ず "I'll take it" を言う前に交渉し、何が欲しいかを具体的に伝えましょう。

[1] to throw in　無料で追加する
[2] a tripod　三脚
[3] with tax...　税込みで
[4] to put on a credit card　カードで支払う

Negotiating prices	
If I buy four, can you give me a better price? (もし四つ買ったら、もう少し安い値段にできますか。)	I could give you 5% off. (5%割り引きはできますが。)
Can you throw in[1] a free T-shirt? (T-シャツを無料で追加できますか。)	No, but I can give you a few souvenir pens. (いいえ、できませんが、何本かのお土産用ペンはあげられます。)

Activity 4 For each situation below, what you would say to the shop clerk to negotiate a better deal?

Situation	You say?
1. You are in a camera shop thinking of buying a $700 camera and a $100 tripod.[2] You also need a lot of film.	
2. You see some $43 (tax included) souvenirs. You have only $200 cash, but you want to buy 5 of them.	

I think that will be all for today（今日は、これで結構です）という表現によって、買い物を終わりにしたいことが伝えられます。すると、店員が会計し、支払いが完了となります。

Activity 5 Work with a partner. Add up the total of the items you bought in Activity 4 above. Calculate any discounts and add 10% tax. Pay the clerk.

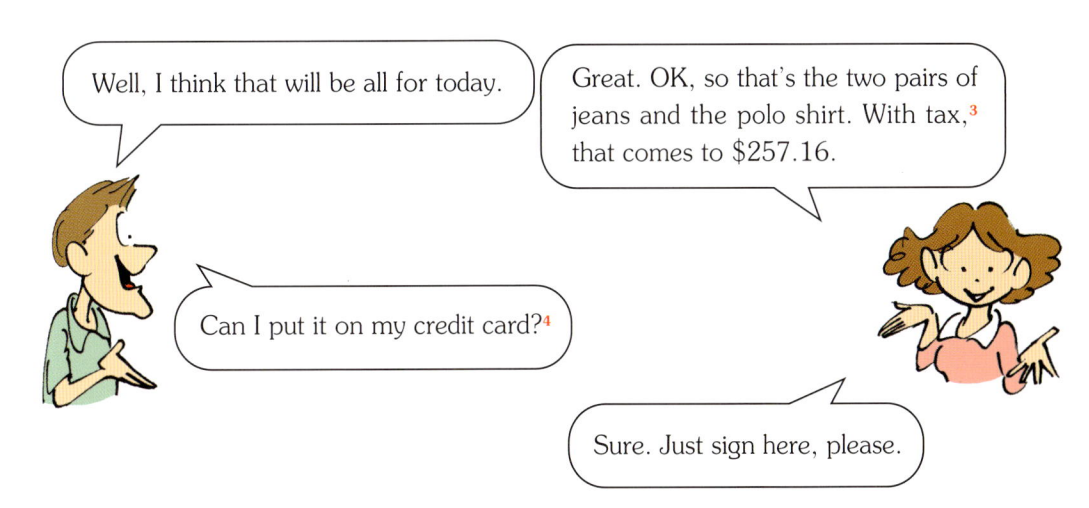

CD 44

Well, I think that will be all for today.

Great. OK, so that's the two pairs of jeans and the polo shirt. With tax,[3] that comes to $257.16.

Can I put it on my credit card?[4]

Sure. Just sign here, please.

Putting It All Together

[1] cologne 香水（男性用）
perfume 香水（女性用）

Role Play: How much is this?

海外で買い物をしています。下の役を交互に、James Bay（お土産）や Wal-Mart（百貨店）でパートナーとショッピングの練習しましょう。

<u>Shopper</u>: 下の商品から好きなものを選び、店員と相談しながら買い物をしましょう。店でたくさん買い物をしたらディスカウントの交渉もしましょう。

<u>Sales clerk</u>: お客さんのショッピングをサポートしましょう。商品を買ってもらうようにお客さんに商品を勧めましょう。

James Bay
Souvenirs

- souvenir t-shirt $24.75
- Native carving Large: $128 Small: $76
- coffee-table book $35
- post cards $1.75 each *or* 5 for $8
- souvenir pins $3 each *or* 2 for $5
- hat $18.75

Wal-Mart
Superstore

- ski boots $634
- jeans $56.50
- dress $188.40
- cologne / perfume [1] $108
- cosmetics kit $44
- iPOD player $349.99
- CD $14.50

練習するとき、レジで10%の消費税で計算しましょう。

Challenge Role Play: It wasn't my fault!

Role Play をもう一回練習しましょう。ただし、今回は、他のお客さんがあなたとぶつかり、あなたの持っていた商品が落ち、壊れてしまいました。そして、そのお客さんが急いで、店から出ていってしまい、店員は、壊れた商品の代金を支払うことを請求します。自分のせいではないことと、自分に代金を支払う責任がないことを店員が納得するように会話をしましょう。

Self-Assessment

Self Assessment Role Play: Over to you!

パートナーと練習してください。このユニットで学んだ内容をもとに、海外でショッピングする設定で、オリジナルロールプレーを作成しましょう。もしクラスあるいは先生の前でロールプレーをする場合、どんな店で買い物をしているかを前もって教えましょう。

下のリストを使い、ロールプレーの自己評価をしてみましょう。上手にできましたか。このユニットで学んだ英語をスムーズに、そして正確に使える自信がつくまで、繰り返し練習しましょう。

Shopping

- [ ] 買いたい商品について店員と相談することができる。
- [ ] 服のサイズについて話ができる。
- [ ] 代わりの商品を注文することができる。
- [ ] 値段の交渉ができる。
- [ ] 支払いすることができる。

Language Focus

- [ ] it's quite loose などの表現を使い、商品について話ができる。
- [ ] a less expensive one などの表現を使い、代わりの商品を注文できる。
- [ ] 買い物だけではなく、様々な意見を言うときなどに、このユニットの language focus が使える。

Vocabulary

次の単語や表現を使える、発音することができる:

- [ ] to fit
- [ ] loose
- [ ] to try on
- [ ] I can't afford it.
- [ ] I'll take it.
- [ ] a carving
- [ ] each
- [ ] a lighter color
- [ ] better
- [ ] to throw in

9 Are You Free Tomorrow?

Have you ever spoken in English over the telephone?

What do you say when you answer the telephone in English?

Where would you invite a new friend in Japan?

ユニット7では、道を尋ねたとき、新しい友人ができました。今回は、その人に電話をし、一緒に遊びに行くように誘います。このユニットでは、電話で人を誘い、会う約束をして、そして簡単な道案内もできるように練習します。

Warm Up…

Mai は、Unit 7 で道を教えてくれた Daniel に電話します。会話を聞き、次の質問に答えましょう。

Question 1: Daniel の日程に Mai 達とのスケジュールを記入しましょう。

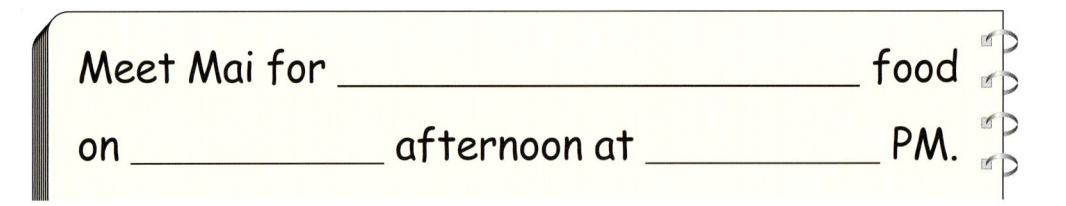

Meet Mai for _____ food
on _____ afternoon at _____ PM.

Question 2: レストランの場所をチェックしましょう。

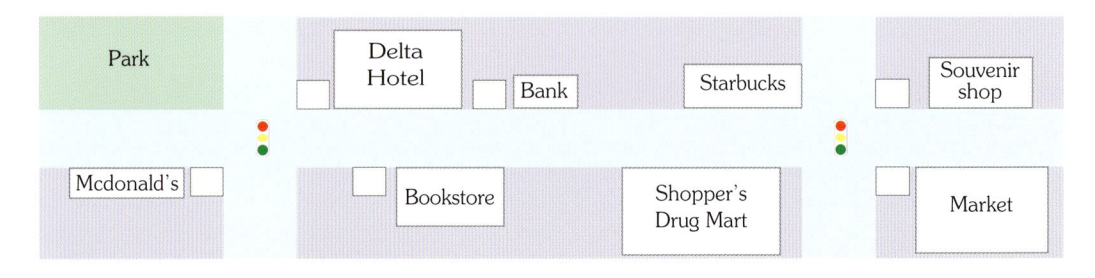

Park		Delta Hotel		Bank		Starbucks		Souvenir shop
Mcdonald's			Bookstore		Shopper's Drug Mart			Market

74 Encounters Abroad

Model Conversation

Inviting

Akaneは、以前に道を教えてくれた人を電話で誘います。(ユニット7を参照)。スケジュールの話をしてから、レストランまでの道を案内します。

Activity 1 Read the conversation below with a partner. Write a memo of the meeting details, including the time, the place, and how to get there.

CD 46

Corey: Hello?
Akane: Hi. Could I[1] speak to Corey Newcomb, please?
Corey: Speaking.[2]
Akane: Hi, Corey. This is[3] Akane Takato. You gave us directions to the museum the other day.[4]
Corey: Oh, yeah.[5] Hi, Akane. How are you? How was the museum?
Akane: Oh, it was fantastic. We loved it. Thanks again[6] for helping us.
Corey: Oh, no problem at all.
Akane: Hey, listen.[7] My friends and I are going out for dinner tomorrow. If you're free,[8] would you like to join us?[9]
Corey: Sure. I'd love to. That sounds great. So...where are you going to go?
Akane: We're planning to go to an Italian restaurant downtown.
Corey: Excellent. I love Italian food. So...what time should I be there?
Akane: How about...uhh...8 o'clock?
Corey: Sure. 8 o'clock is fine. Can you tell me how to get there?
Akane: Yeah. OK. Umm...do you know where the Capital 6 Theater is?
Corey: Uh huh.[10]
Akane: Well, it's just down the street from there, on Rita Road. It's beside a Denny's.
Corey: Oh, yeah. I know that place. OK. Oh, and is it OK if I bring a friend?[11]
Akane: Sure, no problem. The more the merrier![12]
Corey: Great. Thanks. All right, well, I'll see you tomorrow at 8. Thanks for calling.
Akane: Yeah, OK. I'll see you then. Take care. Bye bye.

---

[1] Could I~ 〜していいですか
[2] Speaking. 私ですが。
[3] This is... 〜ですが (電話をかけるほうが言うセリフ)
[4] The other day この間
[5] Oh yeah. (CD音声のイントネーションは、一度忘れた事を思い出す瞬間のもの)
[6] Thanks again for ~ing ありがとう (既にお礼を言ったのに、もう一度お礼を言いたいときに使う表現)
[7] Hey, listen... あのですね。(招待を導入する表現)
[8] If you're free... もし時間があったら
[9] to join 一緒になる/あるグループのメンバーとなる Would you like to join us? 私達と一緒に行きませんか。
[10] Uh huh yesのくだけた言い方
[11] to bring a friend 友達を連れてくる Is it OK if I bring a friend? 友達を連れてきていいですか。
[12] the more the merrier 大勢のほうが楽しい (ことわざ)

現地の人と行動する時、その人が信用できるいい友達になるまでは、レストランやコーヒーショップなど公的な場所で会うほうが安全だということを覚えておきましょう。

Language Focus

Forming embedded questions

道案内をするときや、その他のカジュアルな会話では、**Do you know**（〜かわかりますか）や **Do you remember**（〜を覚えていますか）で始まる質問は役に立ちます。この質問の基本的な単語の順番を覚えるには、下の表を見ましょう。

Do you know where the post office is?
（郵便局はどこにあるか、わかりますか（知っていますか）。）

Do you remember where we ate?
（どこで食べたか、覚えていますか。）

| Do you know / Do you remember | + | where / what / when / the place where / the shop where | + | my hotel / he / the party / we / we | + | is ? / did ? / finished ? / met ? / had coffee ? |

Language Exercise 1：（ ）内の単語を並べ換え、質問を作り、そしてあなた自身の答えを書きましょう。

1. (is / my school / where / do you know)
    Q: _____
    A: _____

2. (do you / why / on Saturday / she / didn't call me / know)
    Q: _____
    A: _____

3. (we / do you / what movie / saw / yesterday / remember)
    Q: _____
    A: _____

4. (what time / are going to meet / do you remember / we / tomorrow)
    Q: _____
    A: _____

Language Exercise 2：次の文章を英語にしましょう。

1. 昨日私達がどこで出会ったか覚えていますか。
    _____

2. Granville Market は、どこにあるかわかりますか。
    _____

3. 私達がどこで車を借りたか覚えていますか。
    _____

4. あの店は、何時に閉まるかわかりますか。
    _____

Language Focus

Giving simple directions

電話で道案内をするときは、まず *Do you know* や *Do you remember* を使い、相手が知っている場所を出発点として設定し、その場所から簡単な道案内しましょう。

> Do you know where Starbucks is?
> (Starbucks はどこにあるか、わかりますか。)

> Well, the restaurant is…
> (じゃあ、レストランは…にあります。)

Giving simple directions	
just across the street from there. (そこから、すぐ反対側の道)	just around the corner. (角を曲がってすぐ)
just down the street. (道を少し歩いたところ)	just beside there. (すぐ隣)

Language Exercise 3: 下の地図を使い、**A - E** の待ち合わせ場所までの道を教えましょう。6問目は、地図から **A - E** 以外の二ケ所を選び、自分の考えで例を書いてください。

1. Do you know where Chapters Books is?

    Well, the restaurant (**A**) is _____

2. Do you remember the rent-a-car place where we met last week?

    The bar (**B**) is _____

3. Do you remember where we had coffee by the beach on Tuesday?

    Well, the movie theater (**C**) is _____

4. _____

    The tennis court (**D**) is just across the street from there.

5. _____

    Well, the club (**E**) is just down the street from there.

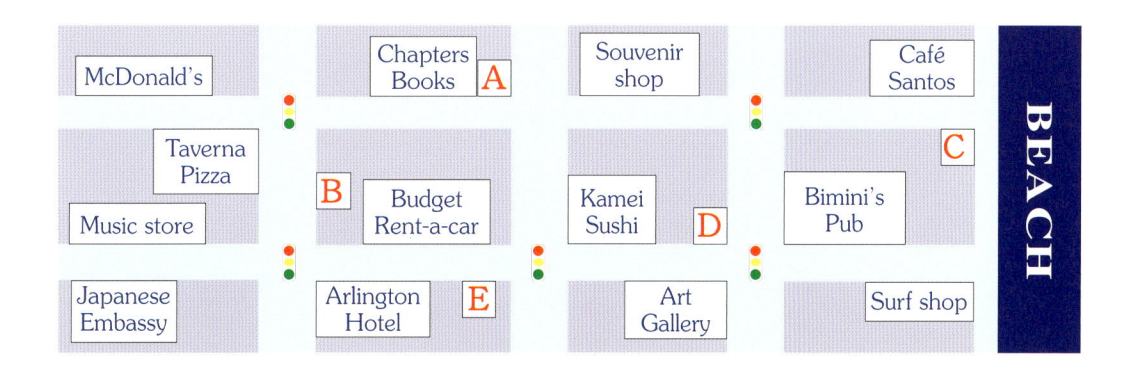

6. _____
    _____

Unit 9 77

Communication Focus

Inviting a new friend

一度しか会っていない人に電話をする時は、自分は誰で、どこで知り合ったかを説明しましょう。

[1] Would you like to...
 〜しませんか。
 Would you like to go? 行きませんか。

CD 47

Hello?

Speaking.

Oh, yeah. Hi, Dale. How are you? Did you find that book you wanted?

ring ring

Hi, can I speak to Kami, please?

Hi, Kami. **This is** Dale. **We met** the other day in front of the bookstore.

この時点で、相手を誘いましょう。自分の考えで空欄に誘う言葉を書きましょう。

Listen, if you're free, would you like to[1] go for lunch on Friday?

My friends and I are going to see a movie this weekend. Would you like to join us?

Activity 2
Work with a partner. You met the following people in Japan. Call and invite them out.

1. Name: **Daniel**
   Met: Last Friday night in Harajuku
   Gave directions to Shibuya
   Invite: Go for a beer on Wednesday

2. Name: **Sandra**
   Met: Last week at Starbucks in Nagoya
   Gave sightseeing advice
   Invite: Go shopping Sunday

誘いを受け入れる前に、その誘いについて質問しましょう。

Activity 3
Read the example phrases below. Then repeat Activity 2, using these phrases.

What movie are you going to see?

What restaurant are you planning to go to?

Where are you planning to go surfing?

Sure.
That sounds great.
I'd love to go.

Communication Focus

Arranging details

下の表現を一つ使って、待ち合わせ時間を決めましょう。

Arranging meeting times	
What time should I be there? (何時に行けばいいですか。)	How would 7:30 be? (7:30だったらどうですか。)
What time should we meet? (何時に待ち合わせしましょうか。)	How about 5:30? (5:30はどうですか。)

待ち合わせ場所が知らない所なら、道を尋ねましょう。

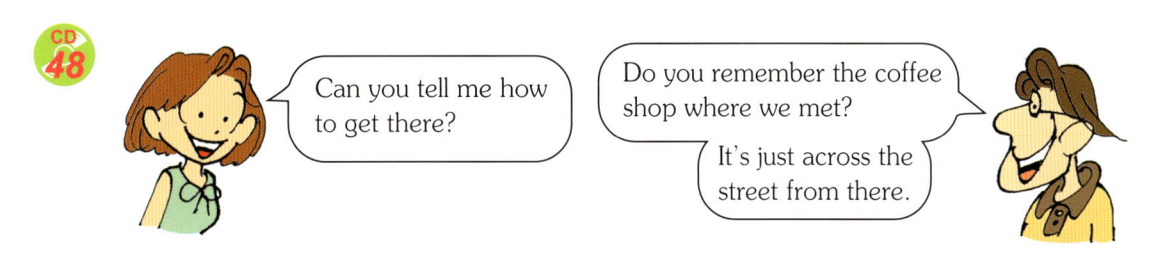

Can you tell me how to get there?

Do you remember the coffee shop where we met? It's just across the street from there.

Activity 4 Invite your partner out to dinner or to go bowling at the times and places shown below. Arrange the time and give directions based on the map.

1. **Place**: Taverna Pizza
   Meet: 7:00

2. **Place**: Rainbow Lanes bowling alley
   Meet: 4:30

Starbucks | Bus Station
Taverna Pizza | Public Library | Bowling Alley

この時点で、最終的な詳細を決め、友達にお礼を言い、電話の会話を終わりにしましょう。

Is it OK if I bring a friend?

See you on Wednesday.

OK, thanks for calling.

OK, bye bye.

Putting It All Together

Role Play: Are you free tomorrow?

新しい友達を誘います。下の役を交互に、Situation 1 and 2 をパートナーと練習しましょう。

<u>Japanese tourist</u>: 下の写真から一つ選び、友人に電話し（緑欄を参考）、でかけるように誘いましょう。会う時間や日程を決め、道案内には、下の地図を使いましょう。

<u>Foreigner</u>: あなたは、この町を詳しく知らないので、誘われたら待ち合わせ場所までの道を尋ねましょう。

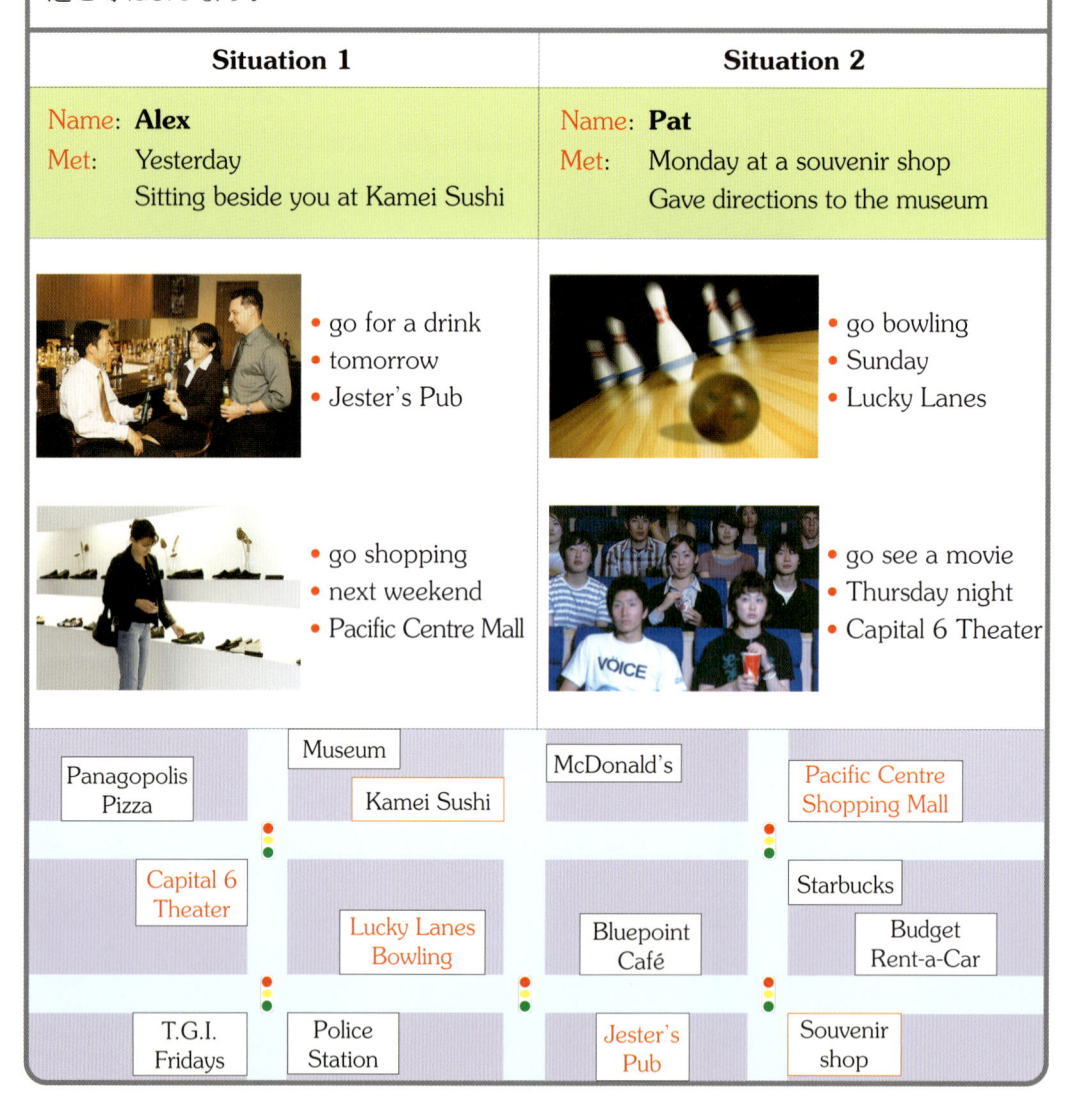

Situation 1

Name: **Alex**
Met: Yesterday
      Sitting beside you at Kamei Sushi

- go for a drink
- tomorrow
- Jester's Pub

- go shopping
- next weekend
- Pacific Centre Mall

Situation 2

Name: **Pat**
Met: Monday at a souvenir shop
      Gave directions to the museum

- go bowling
- Sunday
- Lucky Lanes

- go see a movie
- Thursday night
- Capital 6 Theater

Map

Panagopolis Pizza	Museum / Kamei Sushi	McDonald's	Pacific Centre Shopping Mall
Capital 6 Theater	Lucky Lanes Bowling	Bluepoint Café	Starbucks / Budget Rent-a-Car
T.G.I. Fridays	Police Station	Jester's Pub	Souvenir shop

Challenge Role Play: Sorry, but I'm busy this weekend.

Role Play をもう一回練習しましょう。今回は、外国人のほうからあなたに電話がかかってきて誘われますが、その人のことをあまり好きではなく、一緒にでかけたくありません。具体的な理由を言い、その招待を丁寧に断りましょう。

80 Encounters Abroad

Self-Assessment

Self Assessment Role Play: Over to you!

パートナーと練習してください。このユニットで学んだ内容をもとに、最近出会った人を誘う設定で、オリジナルロールプレーを作成しましょう。場所は海外でも日本でも、自由に設定してください。ロールプレーをする前に簡単な地図を作り、先生に渡しましょう。

下のリストを使い、ロールプレーの自己評価をしてみましょう。上手にできましたか。このユニットで学んだ英語をスムーズに、そして正確に使える自信がつくまで、繰り返し練習しましょう。

Inviting

- [ ] 新しい友人に電話をし、自分はだれか教えることができる。
- [ ] 新しい友達を一緒にでかけるよう、誘うことができる。
- [ ] 招待の内容について、質問をすることができる。
- [ ] 集合時間や道順などについて、決めることができる。
- [ ] 電話の会話を終わらせることができる。

Language Focus

- [ ] Do you know / Do you remember で始まる質問を作ることができる。
- [ ] just across the street などの表現を使い、道案内ができる。
- [ ] 招待するときだけではなく、一般的な会話の中で what や when や why などを使い、"Do you know / Do you remember" での質問を作ることができる。

Vocabulary

次の単語や表現を使える、発音することができる：

- [ ] Speaking.
- [ ] the other day
- [ ] Hey, listen…
- [ ] around the corner
- [ ] Do you remember…
- [ ] to join
- [ ] The more the merrier.
- [ ] to bring a friend
- [ ] across the street
- [ ] if you're free

10 I'll Have the Steak

Have you ever eaten out at a restaurant when traveling abroad? If so, what did you have?

What do you think about most when you look at a menu: price, taste or health?

What dish would you most like to order abroad?

レストランでの飲食は、海外旅行者の誰もがやることです。それを目的に旅行する人も少なくありません。このユニットでは、メニューを読み、食事を注文し、そして料理について友達と話し合えるように練習します。

Warm Up...

Maiは友達とレストランにいます。食事を注文し、料理を食べながら、コメントを互いに言い合います。会話を聞き、次の質問に答えましょう。

CD 49

Question 1: MaiとStuartが注文する料理をチェックしましょう。

Menu		
☐ SALMON SUSHI ROLL	☐ SALMON STEAK	☐ CHICKEN WINGS
☐ SHANGHAI STIR FRY	☐ CAESAR SALAD	☐ ONION RINGS
☐ TERIYAKI CHICKEN	☐ CRISPY DRY RIBS	☐ BACON BURGER

Question 2: 料理についてMaiとStuartの意見を下に書きましょう。

Mai's food is _____. It's _____.

Stuart's food is _____, but it's _____.

82 Encounters Abroad

Model Conversation

Ordering dinner

Yasuhiro と Caitlin は、レストランで注文したい料理について話をしています。注文し、料理がきたら、食べながら、その料理について意見を交換します。

Activity 1

Read the conversation below with a partner. What do Yasuhiro and Caitlin order to eat? Do they like their food?

Yasuhiro: So...what are you going to have?

Caitlin: Well, the salmon looks good. It's a little expensive, but I want something healthy.[1] I might have some calamari,[2] too. How about you? What are you going to have?

Yasuhiro: Hmm...I'm not sure. Let's see. Well, it's a little fattening,[3] but I think I'll have the fish and chips. And I might have some onion rings, too.

Waiter: Hi. May I take your order?[4]

Caitlin: Yes, I'll start with[5] the calamari, and then I'll have the salmon, please.

Waiter: Calamari and salmon. Yes, ma'am. And for you, sir?

Yasuhiro: I'll start with some onion rings, and then could I have the fish and chips, please?

Waiter: OK. Onion rings and the fish and chips. Will that be all,[6] sir?

Yasuhiro: Yeah, that's all for now,[7] thanks.

Waiter: I'll be right back with your appetizers.[8]

Waiter: Here's your calamari, ma'am, and your onion rings, sir. The rest of[9] your order will be right up.[10]

Caitlin: Wow, you should try this calamari. It's excellent. How are the onion rings?

Yasuhiro: Actually, they're not very good. They're kind of greasy.[11] Do you want to trade?[12]

Caitlin: No, thanks. I'll stick with[13] my calamari. Here, try some.

Yasuhiro: Wow. This *is* good!

Caitlin: See. I told ya.

---

[1] healthy 健康的
[2] calamari 輪切りにしたイカに衣をつけて揚げたもの
[3] fattening カロリーが高い
[4] May I take your order? 御注文をどうぞ。
[5] I'll start with... まず〜から（前菜を注文するときのセリフ）
[6] Will that be all? 御注文は以上でよろしいですか。
[7] That's all for now. 取りあえずこれで。
[8] an appetizer 前菜
[9] the rest of〜 その残りの分
[10] ...will be right up 〜をすぐに出します（レストラン用語）
[11] greasy 油っぽい
kind of greasy 少し油っぽい
[12] to trade 交換する
Do you want to trade? 交換しますか。
[13] to stick with 変更無しで、このままで

Language Focus

Reading menus

日本のレストランでは、寿司や焼きそばのように料理の名前をそのままメニューに載せます。しかし、西欧の国では、レストランがメニューに特別な名前をつけることがよくあります。料理の内容を理解するには、各メニューの下にある説明をよく読みましょう。

[1] a starter 前菜
（丁寧な場合は、starter よりも appetizer のほうが適切）

[2] deep fried 油で揚げた

[3] レストランの場合、値段は、「$」印無しで書かれている場合もある。

[4] to serve with 一緒に出る料理（おかず）

[5] an entrée メイン（北米）

[6] chips フライドポテト（イギリス英語）

[7] a ~ stir fry ～炒め
a chicken stir fry チキン炒め
to stir fry 炒める

[8] a jumbo prawn 伊勢エビ
（jumbo は、巨大という意味）

[9] grilled 焼いてある
grilled fish 焼き魚

[10] french fries フライドポテト（北米英語）

[11] unhealthy 健康的でない

starters[1]

CRISPY CRUNCHY RIBS   5.99[3]
Pork rib pieces, deep fried[2] and tossed in our special spicy seasoning.

CAESAR SALAD   5.99
The usual salad served in our unusual way with double-garlic croutons.

GUACAMOLE GUSTO   7.99
Fresh avocado mixed with lemon, tomato and chilis. Made right at your table. Served with[4] tortilla chips.

CRAZY CALAMARI   6.99
Breaded, deep-fried calamari served with tartar sauce and our super special spicy lemon dip.

entrées[5]

CHICKEN TENDERS   7.99
Crisp breaded chicken strips served with honey mustard sauce.

WEST COAST SALMON   17.99
A fillet of local salmon, grilled[9] and served with fresh garden vegetables.

FRESH CAUGHT FISH n' CHIPS[6]   8.99
Deep fried halibut, served with large-cut chips and tartar sauce.

PENNE ARRABBIATA   14.99
For those who like it hot! Penne pasta with our super spicy arrabbiata sauce.

SHANGHAI STYLE STIR FRY[7]   7.99
Jumbo prawns[8] and vegetables sautéed in ginger, garlic and soy. Served over brown rice.

TRIPLE-BYPASS BURGER   14.99
Three beef patties with bacon, three types of cheese and all the fixings. Served with french fries[10]

Language Exercise 1: 上のメニューを読みましょう。健康的なメニューアイテムや体に悪そうなメニューアイテムはどれでしょう。その4つを選び、次の表を完成させましょう。

Healthy dishes	1.	2.
Fattening or unhealthy[11] dishes	3.	4.

Language Exercise 2: 自分が注文したいメニューアイテムを上から2つ書きましょう。

1. _____

2. _____

Language Focus

¹ a plate of... 一皿の〜
² a bowl of... 〜ボウル一杯
³ with dinner 食事中
　after dinner 食後
　before dinner 食前

Using the, a and some with menu items

Use the for specific items:

The は、特別なものや独特なものについて話すときに使います。レストランの場合は、特別な名前を持つ料理（飲み物以外）を注文するとき、the が使われます。

Yes, I'll have **the** Thai stir fry and **the** spaghetti Alfredo.

Use a for general items:

A (an)は、一般的なメニューアイテム(a steak)を注文するときや、料理の単位で(a cup of, a plate of¹) 注文するときに使われます。

Yes, could I have **a** cheeseburger and **a** plate of chicken wings? And could I have **a** glass of water?

Use some for uncountable items:

Some は、単位で数えない料理を注文するときに使われます。

Could I have **some** water, please? And can I have **some** more coffee and **some** sugar, too, please?

飲み物を注文する際、単位を省略することはよくあります。

I'll have **a cup of** coffee.　→　I'll have **a** coffee.
I'll have **a bottle of** beer.　→　I'll have **a** beer.

Language Exercise 3: 下のメニューに **the** や **a**、**some** を書きましょう。

1. _____ piece of apple pie
2. _____ French-onion soup
3. _____ Thai-style fried chicken
4. _____ bacon burger
5. _____ large coffee
6. _____ chocolate ice cream
7. _____ beer
8. _____ french fries
9. _____ BC salmon fillet
10. _____ fish and chips

Language Exercise 4: **The** や **a**、**some** を使い、下の空欄を埋めましょう。2番には、84頁のメニューを参考にしながら、自分の注文を書いてください。

1. I'll have _____ beer and _____ onion rings and _____ bowl of² soup to start with. Then, could I have _____ chicken stir fry? Also, I'd like _____ coffee with dinner,³ please.

2. I'll have...

Communication Focus

[1] **to have** 食べる／飲む
What are you going to have?
= What are you going to eat?

[2] **are you ready to order**
御注文はお決まりでしょうか。

Deciding what to order

友達と食事をする場合は、料理を注文する前に、メニューについて少し話をするでしょう。

Deciding what to order	
Well, the chicken looks (good / healthy). （チキンは、（美味し／健康的）そうですが。）	I might have that. （それにしようかな。）
The lasagna is a little (fattening / expensive). （ラザニヤはちょっと（カロリーが高い／値段が高い）ですが。）	but I think I'll have it anyway. （でも、それにすると思います。）

Activity 2 Study the sample conversation below. Then work in groups of three. Use the menu on page 84 and talk about the foods you are thinking of ordering.

CD 52

— So...what are you going to have?[1]

— Let's see. Well, the pasta looks good. I might have that. How about you? What are you going to have?

Ordering food

次の表現を使い、料理や飲み物を注文できます。

— **I'll start with** a salad.
（まずは、前菜でサラダをお願いします。）

— Then **I'll have** the lasagna.
（そして、ラザニヤをお願いします。）

— And **could I have** **another** coffee, **please**?
（そして、コーヒーをもう一杯頂けますか。）

Activity 3 Use the menu on page 84 to choose appetizers and dinner items, then complete the conversation below. Practice reading your conversation with two partners.

— Are you ready to order?[2]

— Yeah, I'll start with...
Then could I have...

— And for you, Sir?

— Yes, I'll have...

— Will that be all?
OK. I'll be right back with your order.

86 Encounters Abroad

Communication Focus

Talking about food

同伴者に料理の感想を尋ねたほうが礼儀正しいものです。

1 **Why don't you...** ~すれば？（相手にアドバイスをする時に使う）
2 **to complain** 文句を言う
Why don't you complain? 文句を言えば。
3 **It's not that bad.** そんなに悪くない。
4 **Try some.** どうぞ、試してみてください。

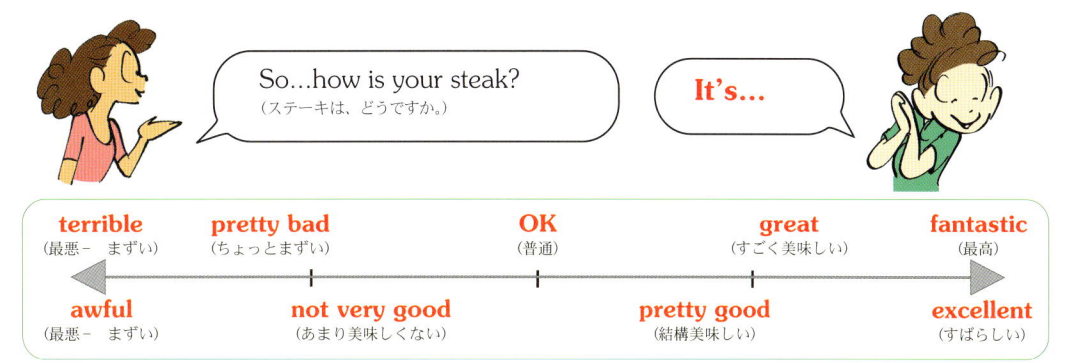

CD 53

So...how is your steak?
(ステーキは、どうですか。)

It's...

terrible (最悪- まずい)	pretty bad (ちょっとまずい)	OK (普通)	great (すごく美味しい)	fantastic (最高)
awful (最悪- まずい)	not very good (あまり美味しくない)		pretty good (結構美味しい)	excellent (すばらしい)

英語では、文句を言う際に、その理由も必ず言います。例えば、その料理が好きでなければ、味や調理法について具体的なコメントも伝えましょう。

It's kind of...
It's a little...
It's really...
It's a bit...

stale (湿気ている)
overcooked (火が通りすぎ)
chewy (噛み切れない)
bitter (苦い)
salty (しょっぱい)
undercooked (火が十分通っていない)
greasy (油っぽい)

Activity 4
Complete the conversation below with the expressions above.

Waiter: Here is your stir fry. And here is your steak, sir. Enjoy your meal.

John: Thanks. So..._____ your stir fry?

Jason: _____ .

John: Why don't you¹ complain?² Tell them you want a new one.

Jason: No, that's OK. It's not *that*³ bad. How about you? _____ steak?

John: _____ ! Here. Try some.⁴

Jason: Wow, this _____ !

Activity 5
Work with one or two partners. Each partner will choose one of the foods below. Take turns asking and giving opinions about your food.

steak　　**spaghetti**　　**fish and chips**

Unit 10 87

Putting It All Together

Role Play: I'll have the steak.

あなたは、友達と食事をしています。3人以上のグループを作り、次の役を交互に練習しましょう。もっとRole Playを難しくするのに、注文する前に、飲み物も注文しましょう。

<u>Customers</u>: 84頁のmenuと下の **specials** メニューを使い、料理を注文しましょう。友達に料理に対しての意見を尋ねたり、自分の料理への意見を言ったりしましょう。

<u>Waiter</u>: 注文を尋ね、料理を運び、質問をされたら、なるべく答えましょう。

LUCIFER'S BAR AND GRILL
On Thurlow

Summer Specials
Get 'em while they're hot!

appetizers

DOUBLE CHEESE BREAD $5.99
Two panini bread loaves filled with garlic and two types of cheese.

THAI GINGER BEEF $8.99
Tender beef cuts tossed in a spicy Thai ginger glaze.

PEPPER PRAWNS $9.99
Four jumbo prawns sautéed with red and green peppers, garlic, and black pepper.

entrées

HELL-BROILED BURGER $14.99
Our world famous flame-broiled burger with grilled onions and hot sauce. Served with french fries.

EAST COAST LOBSTER $27.99
Fresh from the Atlantic to your table. Served with seasonal vegetables and garlic butter dip. And a bib, of course.

SPICY VEGGIE VIETNAM $11.99
Fresh seasonal vegetables and tofu sautéed in white wine, with Vietnamese herbs and spices.

Challenge Role Play: Can I speak to the manager, please?

Role Playをもう一回練習しましょう。ただし、今回は、注文と違う料理が届き、そのミスによってオーダーが15分よけいにかかります。それに、オーダーが届いたら、長い髪の毛一本を発見！マネージャーを呼んで、文句を言いましょう。料理が無料になるだけでなく、皆がフリードリンク一杯をもらえるように苦情を言いましょう。

Self-Assessment

Self Assessment Role Play: *Over to you!*

3人以上のグループで練習しましょう。このユニットで学んだ内容をもとに、レストランで食べる設定で、オリジナルロールプレーを作成しましょう。レストランは海外でも国内でも構いません。メニューは、自分で作るか、インターネットからダウンロードするか、このユニットにあるメニューを使っても構いません。

下のリストを使い、ロールプレーの自己評価をしてみましょう。上手にできましたか。このユニットで学んだ英語をスムーズに、そして正確に使える自信がつくまで、繰り返し練習しましょう。

Ordering Dinner

- ☐ 注文する前に友達とメニューについて話ができる。
- ☐ レストランでお客さんの注文を受けることができる。
- ☐ 前菜とメインを注文することができる。
- ☐ 注文した料理について意見を求めたり、言ったりすることができる。

Language Focus

- ☐ 英語で書いたメニューを読んだり、使うことができる。
- ☐ 注文するとき the、a、some を適切に使うことができる。
- ☐ the、a、some の一般的な使い方をさらに理解できた。

Vocabulary

次の単語や表現を使える、発音することができる:

- ☐ greasy
- ☐ healthy
- ☐ a stir fry
- ☐ fattening
- ☐ I'll have…
- ☐ And for you?
- ☐ I'll start with…
- ☐ an appetizer
- ☐ to be right up
- ☐ an entrée

Unit Review 2

Extended role play

A trip to San Francisco

一回目のレビューでは、Los Angeles への旅行しました。今回の Unit 6 - 10 のレビューでは、Los Angeles から San Francisco にある Fisherman's Wharf への小旅行をします。

4人組のグループで練習してください。2人は、観光客（**travelers**）の役をし、**全部**のロールプレーをしなければなりません。他の2人は、レンタル店のクラークなど、サポートの役をします。正確な英語よりも、自分なりに楽しんで、各シチュエーションをクリアするよう、頑張ってください。

Travelers
(*Students 1 & 2*)

Car Rental — San Francisco での3日間の旅のため、Los Angeles で、91頁の Rental Agreement を記入し、車をレンタルしましょう。

Directions — 91頁の地図から行き先を選び、泊まっているホテルのすぐ外で（**Start**）、道を尋ねましょう。

Shopping — 91頁からのアイテムを使い、Souvenir ショッピングをしましょう。

Inviting — あなたと友達との外食に、道を教えてくれた人を誘いましょう。場所は *Joe's Crab Shack*（91項の地図に参考）。

Dinner — 一人は、ウェーターの役にし、91頁のメニューを使い、残り三人は *Joe's Crab Shack* で皆で食べましょう。

90 Encounters Abroad

Rental agreement

LA Rentals

Client Information:
1. Name: _____
2. Address: Street _____
   City _____ Province/State _____
   Country _____ Postal Code _____
3. Rental Period: From (dd/mm/yr) _____ To _____

Insurance:
Please indicate and initial for an insurance option.

- Full coverage: $22.22 / day ☐
- Full coverage declined ☐   Renter Initials: X _____

I have read and agree to the terms of this agreement.
Customer Signature: X _____

Menu

JOE'S CRAB SHACK

245 Jefferson St,
San Francisco
Between Taylor & Jones

Appetizers

Clam Chowder. 6.49
New England Style

Peel n' Eat Shrimp. 8.49
You peel 'em! Baker's dozen

Crab Stuffed Mushrooms. . 6.99
Stuffed with fresh seafood

Joe's Crispy Calamari. . . . 6.99
250g of Calamari, lightly fried

Awesome Appetizer. . . . 12.99
Boiled shrimp, crap dip & potato skins

Crabs, Crabs and More Crabs!

BBQ Dungeness Crab (600g) 24.99
Fresh from the Northwest

Snow Crab . . . . .(600g) 19.99
Direct from the North Atlantic

Crab Daddy Feast. 27.99
King, Dungeness and Snow

Steak, Chicken and Pasta

Sirloin Steak (10oz) . . .16.99
A steak lover's favorite

Teriyaki Chicken Breast . .12.99
Tender, juicy, healthy

Jumbo Shrimp Pasta 13.99
Pasta with parmesan breaded shrimp

Shopping

- coffee-table book — $49.99
- toy cable-car — $38
- souvenir mug — $14 or 2 for $25
- souvenir plate — $25 or 3 for $60
- t-shirt — $34

Directions

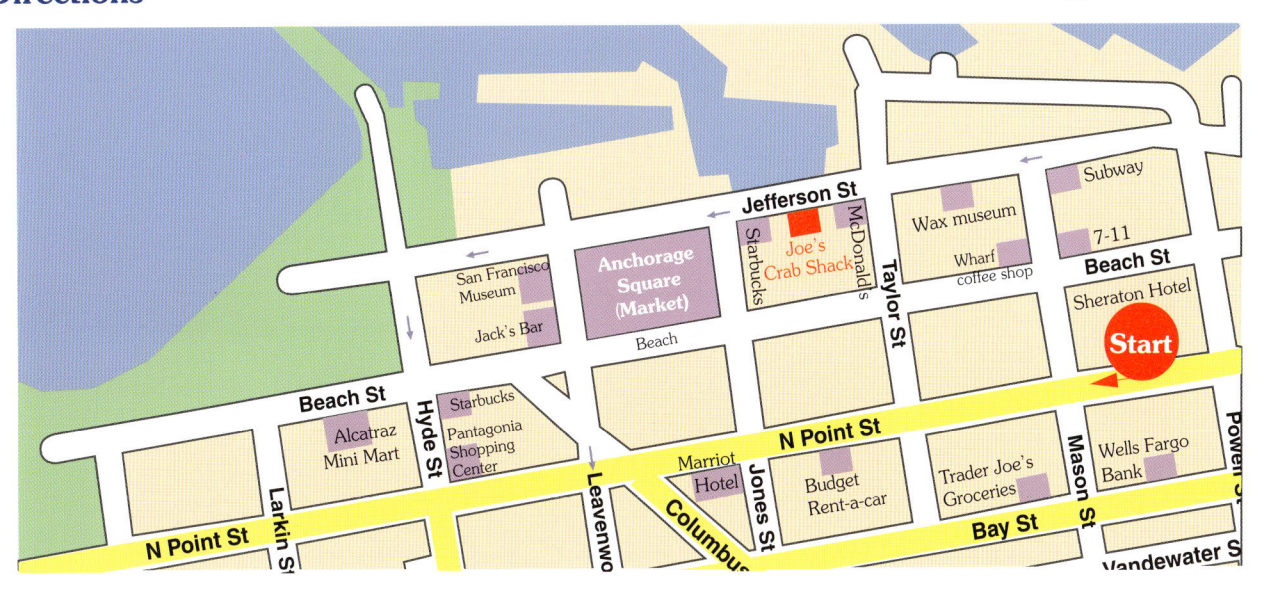

Transcripts

Unit 1: Where Are You Heading?
Mai: Excuse me. Is it OK if I sit here?
Bob: Sure, no problem.
M: Thanks. I hope we can board the plane soon. I want to get going.
B: Yeah, me, too. So...are you going to visit Vancouver?
M: Actually, I'm going to live there. I'll be there for three months.
B: Three months? Wow. That's a long time. So...what are you planning to do in Vancouver?
M: I'm going to study English.
B: Really? Cool. So...what school are you going to go to?
M: It's a language school downtown. It's called Pacific Gateway.
B: Great. Good for you. So...are you planning to do any sightseeing?
M: Yeah, I plan to travel before school starts. Actually, I'm going to visit a friend next week.
B: Oh, yeah. So...what are you and your friend planning to do?
M: Well, my friend loves fishing, so we're going to go salmon fishing.
B: Fishing? That'll be fun. I hope you catch a big one.
M: Thanks. So...are you from Vancouver?
B: No, I'm from a place called Whiterock. It's about an hour south of Vancouver.
M: I see. So...what do you do?
B: I work in a bank. How about you? What do you do?
M: Oh, I'm a student.
B: Oh, yeah? What do you study?
M: International communication.
B: International communication? Wow. That sounds interesting. So...do you study in Tokyo?
M: Yeah, I do, but I live in Ageo City. It's just north of Tokyo.
B: Yeah, I know Ageo. I was staying with a friend there.
M: No way! Really? So...how did you like Saitama?
B: Oh, it was great. The people are really nice there.
M: I'm glad to hear that you liked it. By the way, my name is Mai.
B: Hi, Mai. I'm Bob. It's nice to meet you.
M: Yeah, nice to meet you, too.
B: OK, time to go.

Unit 2: May I See Your Passport?
Officer: Next. Good morning. May I see your passport and your landing card, please?
Mai: Yes, here they are.
O: Thank you. And what is the purpose of your visit to Canada?
M: I'm here to study English.
O: OK. I see your visa here. And what is the name of your school?
M: It's called Pacific Gateway.
O: Do you have the address?
M: I'm sorry. Could you repeat that, please?
O: Do you have the address? The address of the school?
M: Oh. Yes. It's on Robson Street. 1155 Robson Street. Here's my e-mail from them.
O: OK, thank you. And how long will you be staying in Canada?
M: I'll be here for 3 months.
O: 3 months? OK. And where will you be staying?
M: I'll be staying at a hotel for a few nights, then I'll be staying with a homestay family.
O: And what do you do in Japan, ma'am?
M: I'm a student.
O: A student? I see. And are you carrying any fruits or vegetables with you?
M: No. But I do have some souvenirs with me.
O: Oh, that's no problem. OK, please show your landing card to the customs officer on your way out. Welcome to Canada.
M: Thank you.
O: Good luck with your school.
M: Thanks. Have a good day.

Unit 3: Where To?
Driver: Here. Let me help you with your luggage.
Mai: Thanks.
D: So...where to?
M: Could you take me to the Wenman Hotel, please?
D: That's the place on Arbutus, right?
M: Yeah, I think so.
D: OK.

M: Wow. Kamei Sushi? That must be a Japanese restaurant.
D: Yeah, that's right. There are about 4 Kamei Sushi restaurants in town now. It's really popular.
M: So...Canadian people like Japanese food?
D: Oh, yeah. There are Japanese restaurants everywhere now. So...are you from Japan?
M: Yeah. From the Tokyo area.
D: Ahh...my sister is living in Tokyo now.
M: Really? What does she do there?
D: She works at a university.
M: Oh, that's great. I hope she likes it there.
D: Oh, yeah, she loves it. So...how long was your flight today?
M: 10 hours! I'm so tired. Actually, is there a Starbucks or something on the way? I would really love to get a coffee.
D: Sure, there's a Starbucks on the corner of Broadway and Arbutus. I can stop there if you want.
M: Oh, yes, please. That would be great. Thanks.
D: OK, here's the Starbucks.
M: Great. I'll be right back. Hey, you've been so nice. Can I get you a coffee?
D: Really? Thanks. I'd love one. Just a black coffee would be fine, thanks.
M: OK, I'll be right back.

M: Thanks for waiting. Here's your coffee.
D: Thanks. The hotel is just up the street here.

D: OK, here's the hotel.
M: Great. Thanks. How much is the fare?
D: That'll be $24.00, please.
M: $24.00? OK. Umm...let me see. Here's $30. Keep the change.
D: Well, that's very nice of you. A *coffee* and a $6 tip. Thanks very much.
M: You're welcome. No problem.
D: I hope you have a great trip.
M: Well, it's starting out good. Thanks for the ride.

Unit 4: I Asked for a Double
Reception: Good morning. Welcome to the Wenman Hotel.
Mai: Hi. I have a reservation for Mai Ichiyama.
R: Let me check. Oh, yes, Ms. Ichiyama. We have you booked for a single room for 3 nights on a non-smoking floor, as you requested.
M: What? Umm...actually, on the Internet, I asked for *four* nights. And I wanted a *double* room. Here's a copy of my reservation.
R: Oh, I see. I'm sorry about the mix-up. So you wanted a

Transcripts

double room?
M: Yes, a double room.
R: I see. And you plan to stay *four* nights? So you'll be checking out on July 26th, then?
M: Yes, that's correct. I'll be leaving on July 26th.
R: OK. I'll change that for you right away. All right. So that's four nights in a double room. I'm *so* sorry about the mistake.
M: Oh, that's all right. No problem.
R: OK, uhh...could you fill out and sign this check-in card, please?
M: All right. Here you go.
R: Thank you very much. OK. Here's your key. You're in room 1253.
M: Thanks. Oh, by the way, on the Internet I read that you have a fitness center. Where is it?
R: Yes, the fitness center is on the fourth floor. It's beside the swimming pool.
M: Beside the swimming pool? OK, great. And what time does it open?
R: The fitness room opens at 7:30 AM and it closes at 10 PM.
M: OK, so 7:30 to 10 PM. Umm...how much does it cost?
R: How much? Oh, guests can use the fitness room for *free*. There's no charge. But you do need to wear proper footwear.
M: Footwear? You mean running shoes?
R: Yes, ma'am. Any kind of running shoe or sports shoe is OK.
M: Oh. No problem. I brought everything I need. So I'm in room 1253, right?
R: Yes, that's correct.
M: Thanks very much.
R: Enjoy your stay.

Unit 5: What Would You Suggest? (CD 22)

Mai: Good morning.
Concierge: Good morning. How can I help you today?
M: Umm...I've got some free time tomorrow and I want to do some sightseeing around Vancouver. What would you suggest?
C: Well, what kinds of things would you like to do?
M: Well, I'd like to spend some time doing things that the local people do. You know, just normal things that Canadians do. Oh! And also, I'd like to try some of the local food.
C: OK. Well, then, I'd suggest that you start the day at Granville Island Market. It's a popular place with local people. It has a lot of good shops, and it's a *great* place to have lunch.
M: That sounds great. What time does the market open?
C: Well, the shops open at about 9 in the morning.
M: All right. I think I'll do that. What about in the afternoon?
C: Well, in the afternoon, I'd suggest that you go downtown. You could start off by visiting Stanley Park. It's right downtown and it's a great way to spend the afternoon. And they have a very nice aquarium there, too.
M: An aquarium? Cool. How much does it cost to see that?
C: Oh, let me check. Umm...the aquarium is $18.50 a person.
M: $18.50? That's not bad. Well, maybe I'll do that. So...what about in the evening?
C: The evening? Well, first, for dinner, I'd suggest that you go to one of the restaurants on English Bay.
M: English Bay? Do you mean the restaurant is beside the ocean?
C: That's right. The restaurants there are very good, and at sunset the view is beautiful.

M: Oh, that's a great idea.
C: Then, after dinner, you could walk up Robson Street. It's another really popular area. It has lots of shops and restaurants. If you like shopping, you'll love Robson Street.
M: Yeah, actually, I love to shop. Wow. Thanks very much for the advice. I'm really looking forward to tomorrow.
C: You're more than welcome, ma'am. Actually, here's a map. Let me show you where everything is. Umm...OK...here's Granville Island. Then in the afternoon, you need to go here to the downtown area. And this is Stanley Park. Then in the evening, the restaurants on English Bay are right here. And Robson Street is here.
M: Great. Thanks so much for your help.
C: My pleasure. Have a great day tomorrow.
M: I will. Thanks.

Unit 6: Here Are Your Keys (CD 28)

Clerk: Hi. How are you today?
Mai: Good, thanks. I'd like to rent a car for five days, please.
C: Five days? All right. And what kind of car do you need, ma'am?
M: Well, we need a car for two people, my friend and I, and we have a lot of luggage. Umm...how much are your economy cars?
C: Our economy cars are $24.50 a day. But for two people...if you have a lot of luggage...it might be a little small.
M: All right, well, how much is a mid-size car?
C: Our mid-size rate is $35.00 a day. But if you rent for more than 3 days, we can give you 15% off. So that would be $29.75 a day.
M: Wow. That's a great price. OK, I think I'll take the mid-size car, then.
C: A mid-size? All right. And do you need insurance? Our insurance is $18.50 per day.
M: Yeah, I think I need insurance. I'm not used to driving in Canada.
C: All right, then. Let me see. That's a mid-size car, at $29.75 a day, for 5 days. OK, with insurance and tax, your total rental cost is $275.03.
M: $273.03? OK, here's my credit card.
C: Thanks. And can you fill out this form, please?
M: Sure.
C: And may I see your passport and your international driver's license, please?
M: All right. Here you go.
C: OK. Here's your card back, ma'am. Now let's go outside and check the car.

Unit 7: Turn Left at the Light (CD 32)

Mai: Excuse me.
Daniel: Yes?
M: Uhh...I'm trying to find the bus station. Could you tell me how to get there?
D: The bus station? Sure. It's easy. Uhh...can you see the Starbucks there?
M: Yeah, I can see it.
D: OK, turn left at that Starbucks, and walk for a few minutes, and you'll see a Denny's on your left.
M: A Denny's? All right.
D: OK. Just turn right at the Denny's and you'll see the bus

93

Transcripts

    station on your left.
M: So the bus station is on the left. OK, got it. Thanks very much.
D: Sure. No problem. So...are you going on a trip?
M: Yeah, I'm going to visit a friend in Port Alberni.
D: Port Alberni? No way. Really? That's where I'm from.
M: Are you serious?
D: Yeah. So...you have a friend in Port Alberni?
M: Actually, it's my old English teacher. I'm going to go and visit her for a few days and, you know, do some sightseeing.
D: Great. Well, I think you'll like it. It's a small town, but there's a lot to do there.
M: Great. So...do you live in Vancouver now?
D: Uh huh.
M: What do you do here?
D: Oh, I'm a student. I go to university here.
M: Oh, yeah. What's your major?
D: I'm studying economics.
M: Economics? Cool. Actually, I'm a student, too. I'm Mai, by the way.
D: Hi, Mai. I'm Daniel. Nice to meet you. Actually, here's my number. Give me a call when you get back from Port Alberni. I'd love to show you around Vancouver.
M: Oh, I'd love that. That's very nice of you. Thanks.
D: No problem. Listen, I have to go. I have to get to class. Have a great trip.
M: OK, thanks, Daniel. Have a great day. See ya.

Unit 7: Turn Left at the Light.
Map scripts Page 62, Activity 2

(***Narration voice***: *Listen to the directions. Write them on the map as you hear them. Then circle the final destination. Conversation 1.*)
Japanese: Excuse me. We're trying to find some (*beeeep*). Could you tell us where we can find some?
Foreigner: Sure. Uhh...can you see the Starbucks there?
J: Uhh....uh-huh, yeah.
F: OK, turn left at that Starbucks. Then go straight and you'll see a Denny's on your left.
J: Denny's? All right.
F: OK, turn left at the Denny's, walk for about two minutes and you'll see some on your right.
J: On my right. OK. Thanks very much for your help.
F: My pleasure.

(***Narration voice***: *Conversation 2.*)
Japanese: Excuse me. I wonder if you can help me. I'm a little lost.
Foreigner: Sure. What are you looking for?
J: Well, I'm going to visit a friend at (*beeeep*), but I don't know how to get there.
F: Well, it's a little bit far from here, but it's easy to find.
J: All right.
F: OK, uhh...walk straight along this street for about 10 minutes, and turn left at the...uhh...third traffic light.
J: Left at the third traffic light? OK.
F: Go straight and you'll see a bookstore on the corner. Turn right at the bookstore and you'll see it on your left.
J: On my left. OK. Got it. Thanks.
F: You're welcome.

(***Narration voice***: *Conversation 3.*)
Japanese: Excuse me.
Foreigner: Yes?
J: Umm...I'm trying to find the (*beeeep*). Could you tell me how to get there?
F: Oh, it's easy. Just walk up this street and turn left at the second traffic light. You'll see it on your left.
J: OK, so left at the second light.
F: Yes. Oh, no! Wait a minute. I'm sorry. I forgot. They've closed that street.
J: Oh, no! So...how can I get there?
F: It's all right. There's another way. Uhh...can you see that Starbucks there?
J: The one there? OK.
F: Turn left there at the Starbucks, walk for about a minute and you'll see a 7-Eleven on your right.
J: 7-Eleven, OK.
F: Yeah. Turn right there. Then walk up that little street and you'll see it on your left.
J: OK, so I turn right at the 7-Eleven and then go straight.
F: Yeah, that's right.
J: OK, that seems easy. Thanks for the help.
F: You're quite welcome. I just hope you make it on time. I think they close at noon.
J: No way. Really? I'd better hurry then. Thanks again for the help.
F: No problem. See ya.

Unit 8: How Much Is This?

Mai: Excuse me. Can I try on these shoes?
Clerk: Yes, of course. Here you go. How do they fit?
M: Umm...they're a little tight. Can I try a larger size, please?
C: Sure. OK, these are a size 6 1/2. How do they fit?
M: Oh, they're great. How much are they?
C: They're $170.
M: Well, they're a little expensive, but I really like them. Ahh...all right, I'll take them.
C: Great. Can I help you with anything else today?
M: No, just the shoes, thanks.
C: OK, will that be cash or credit?
M: Cash, please.
C: All right. With tax that comes to $193.80.
M: Here you go.
C: Thank you.
M: Oh, and I want to buy some souvenirs. Do you have a souvenir area in this store?
C: Yes, we do. It's on the first floor, just beside the escalators.
M: Oh, great, thanks.
C: You're welcome. Have a nice day.

C: Good morning. Can I help you?
M: Yes. How much are these souvenir baseball hats?
C: They're $15 each.
M: OK, I'll take 2 of these hats. Oh, and what are these little green things?
C: Oh, those are jade carvings.
M: Hmm...how much are they?
C: They're $112 each.
M: Hmm...they're a little expensive, but they're really beautiful.

Transcripts

Umm...if I buy 3 of these carvings, can you give me a better price?
C: Sorry. Not really. But if you buy 3, I could give you an extra baseball hat for free.
M: Really? That would be great. Thanks. OK, I'll take 3 of these jade carvings, then, please. And I think that will be all for today.
C: All right, so that's the 3 jade carvings, and the 2 baseball hats, with 14% sales tax, that comes to $417.24.
M: 14% sales tax? Wow! That's much higher than in Japan.
C: Yeah, sales tax here is really high now.
M: Yeah, it sure is. I'm sorry. So...what was the total, again?
C: Uhh...that will be $417.24, please.
M: Can I put it on my credit card?
C: Sure, no problem. Just sign here, please. OK, here you go. Thanks for shopping at The Bay.

Unit 9: Are You Free Tomorrow?

Daniel: Hello?
Mai: Hi. Could I speak to Daniel Anderson, please?
D: Speaking.
M: Hi, Daniel. This is Mai Ichiyama. You gave me directions to the bus station the other day. You told me to call you when I got back into Vancouver.
D: Oh, yeah. Hi, Mai. How are you?
M: I'm good, thanks.
D: So...how was Port Alberni?
M: Oh, it was fantastic. I had such a good time.
D: That's great.
M: Hey, listen, Daniel, I'm meeting some friends for lunch on Sunday. If you're free, would you like to join us?
D: Sunday afternoon? Sure. That sounds great. So...where are you planning to go?
M: Well, one of my friends is from Thailand, so we're going to a Thai restaurant downtown.
D: Cool. Actually, I've never tried Thai food, but it sounds great. So...what time should I be there?
M: How about 1:30?
D: 1:30? Sure, that sounds great. Can you tell me how to get to the restaurant?
M: Yeah, sure. Uhh...do you know where the big Shoppers Drug Mart is?
D: The Shoppers Drug Mart? Do you mean the one across the street from Starbucks?
M: Yeah, that's the one. Well, the Thai restaurant is just down the street from there, near the Delta Hotel.
D: Oh, yeah, I know that restaurant. It's beside the bank, right? Kind of across the street from the bookstore.
M: Yeah, that's right. The one beside the Royal Bank.
D: OK. So I'll see you there at around 1:30 on Sunday.
M: All right, I'll see you then.
D: I'm looking forward to hearing about your trip to Port Alberni.
M: OK, I'll tell you all about it.
D: Thanks for calling.
M: OK, bye bye.

Unit 10: I'll Have the Steak

Mai: So...what are you going to have?
Stuart: I'm not sure. The bacon burger looks good, but I want to eat something healthy. Hmm...let's see. Well, the teriyaki chicken looks good, too. I think I might have that. How about you? What are you going to have?
M: I'm not sure. I want to try some local cuisine. What would you suggest?
S: Well, it's a little expensive, but the salmon steak is a typically Canadian food.
M: Wow. $23. That *is* expensive. But I'm on holiday, so who cares, right? OK, I'll have that.
S: Are you going to have an appetizer?
M: An appetizer? Sorry, I don't understand.
S: An appetizer. It's a small dish before your main course. I think the word is *zensai* in Japanese.
M: Ahh! I see. Uhh...well, the chicken wings look a bit fattening, but I think I'll have those. Help me eat them, OK?
S: OK.

Waiter: May I take your order?
Mai: Yes, I'll start with the chicken wings, and then I'll have the salmon steak, please.
Waiter: Chicken wings and the salmon. Yes, ma'am. And for you, sir?
Stuart: Could I have the teriyaki chicken, please.
Waiter: Teriyaki chicken. OK, so that's the chicken wings to start with, then the salmon steak and teriyaki chicken. Great. I'll be back soon with your order.

Waiter: OK, here are your chicken wings. I'll be back in a few minutes with the rest of your order.
Mai: Thanks.
Stuart: So...how are the chicken wings?
M: Actually, they're not very good.
S: Really? You don't like them?
M: Not really. They're a little greasy. And the sauce is too spicy.
S: Greasy and spicy? OK, then you can eat them all yourself.
M: No, help me eat them!
S: OK.

Waiter: All right. Here's your salmon steak and your teriyaki chicken. Enjoy your meal.
Stuart: Thank you.
Mai: So...how is the teriyaki chicken?
S: Well, it's a bit salty, but it's pretty good. I like it.
M: Really? Can I try some?
S: Sure. Here.
M: Mmm...this *is* good. I should have had this, too.

Additional acknowledgements:

For providing high-res photos or logos, my thanks to the following individuals and companies:

Air Canada: *In flight*: Page 8
Chateau Victoria Hotel logo: Page 28 (*Thanks to Brenda Ollis and Jason Partridge*)
St. Mary's University logo: Page 28 (*Thanks to Denis Leclaire and Yi Xie*)
Camosun College logo: Page 30 (*Thanks to Dawn Sutherland*)
HotelClub logo: Page 35 (*Thanks to Mikiya Terauchi   http://www.hotelclub.com*)
Elliot Lowe: *Hockey*: Page 46
Holiday Inn Hotels and Resorts logo: Page 49
Graham Duffield: *Beverly Hills sign*: Page 49
Canada: A Visual Journey. By Tanya Lloyd Kyi: Photo Page 72 courtesy of Whitecap Books (http://www.whitecap.ca). Special thanks to Nadine Boyd.
Nori Suzuki: *Bar scene, Movie scene*: Page 80

For graciously allowing us to photograph on their premises, I would like to express my appreciation to the Chateau Victoria Hotel, Budget Rent-a-Car, James Bay Trading Co. (Thanks to Kim Jones) and the Elephant and Castle Restaurant.

Encounters Abroad [B-539]

すぐ使える海外旅行英語

1 刷	2007年 2月22日	
10 刷	2022年 8月1日	
著 者	Michael P. Critchley	マイケル・クリチェリー
	e-mail: support@encounters.jp	
発行者	南雲 一範 Kazunori Nagumo	
発行所	株式会社 南雲堂 〒162-0801　東京都新宿区山吹町 361 NAN'UN-DO Publishing Co., Ltd. 361 Yamabuki-cho, Shinjuku-ku, Tokyo 162-0801, Japan 振替口座：00160-0-46863 TEL: 03-3268-2311 （代表）／ FAX: 03-3269-2486 編集者　TA / JK / YK	
製版所	スタジオAina	
イラスト	さとう　有作	
検 印	省　略	
コード	ISBN 978-4-523-17539-1 C0082	

Printed in Japan

E-mail　nanundo@post.email.ne.jp
homepage　https://www.nanun-do.co.jp/